RULE THE ROOM

A UNIQUE, PRACTICAL, AND COMPREHENSIVE GUIDE
TO MAKING A SUCCESSFUL PRESENTATION

JASON TETEAK
WITH DALE BURG

NEW YORK

RULE THE ROOM
A UNIQUE, PRACTICAL, AND COMPREHENSIVE GUIDE
TO MAKING A SUCCESSFUL PRESENTATION

ISBN 978-1-61448-613-8 paperback
ISBN 978-1-61448-614-5 eBook
ISBN 978-1-61448-615-2 audio
Library of Congress Control Number: 2013938568

Morgan James Publishing
The Entrepreneurial Publisher
5 Penn Plaza, 23rd Floor,
New York City, New York 10001
(212) 655-5470 office • (516) 908-4496 fax
www.MorganJamesPublishing.com

Cover Design by:
Chris Treccani
www.3dogdesign.net

Interior Design by:
Bonnie Bushman
bonnie@caboodlegraphics.com

In an effort to support local communities, raise awareness and funds, Morgan James Publishing donates a percentage of all book sales for the life of each book to Habitat for Humanity Peninsula and Greater Williamsburg.

Get involved today, visit
www.MorganJamesBuilds.com.

Habitat
for Humanity®
Peninsula and
Greater Williamsburg
Building Partner

To God be all the Glory

TABLE OF CONTENTS

INTRODUCTION

You're about to learn how to create a customized, memorable presentation; feel more prepared and confident; and engage and entertain even the most challenging audience. In more than twenty years of working with people in the corporate and academic worlds, I have seen them struggle with many types of presentation issues. If you have picked up this book, I am sure you can relate to problems such as the following.

> *I have a deep-seated fear of being in front of a large group of people and being publicly humiliated. And I don't know how to deal with issues that aren't conscious. My heart starts beating rapidly, my voice quivers, my palms sweat, and I forget what I'm going to say.*
>
> *I need to make a good impression quickly, impress the audience, and lay a foundation for them to look at me as a leader. I want them to feel engaged, not steamrollered.*
>
> *Being able to sell someone on my ideas is a huge challenge. My company has great potential, but I'm having trouble creating a presentation that makes people clearly understand how it will benefit them.*
>
> *The major driver for me is respect. I want to know how to use communication skills to generate a sense of authority, help me lead a company, and teach my employees the right principles.*

I feel so nervous about losing credibility or failing to get my audience to understand me. I worry I won't know the answers; that I'll look foolish, awkward, or uncomfortable; and, yes, that no one will like me.

Though I've given several hundred presentations to prospective customers and I know they need my services, many times they don't pull the trigger. How can I get them to act?

Keeping some topics interesting is a real challenge. In other cases, the discussions often become heated and difficult to control. I want advice for dealing with the spectrum—how to fire up an audience that isn't engaged and how to cool them down when they're squabbling.

I want to build a brand by speaking at webinars. How can I use just my voice to get people to buy in to what I'm saying?

I love to teach. I would love to travel and motivate large audiences to respond to what I'm telling them. I don't know how.

I am always impressed when presenters come into the room and project confidence from the moment they appear. If it's possible, I want to learn how to look confident.

Our team needs to get better at proving we're a credible and reliable resource that others should partner with. What can we do that will create this impression?

I worry about looking like a deer in the headlights when I get questions that I can't answer or must deflect because they're preventing me from putting across my message.

My problem: coming into a classroom where scores of students are surfing their laptops and cell phones, calling for their attention, and then keeping it while I have to deliver a fire hose of information for a solid hour. Help!

I have responded to countless requests like these. Many of them have come from individuals who have achieved tremendous success yet still had problems getting in front of a group of people and persuading, motivating, teaching, or inspiring so effectively that they would actually change behavior.

I developed Rule the Room to solve their problems. I can solve yours, too.

The immediately actionable advice I give you will help you not only in giving presentations but also in your everyday life. The inner confidence you develop when you become a successful presenter, when you know you can stand up in front of any number of people and hold their attention, gain their respect, earn their applause, and get a response, will be something you carry with you everywhere.

I have given thousands of presentations and appeared before more than one hundred thousand people. I have also worked with hundreds of private clients, observing them, writing up to five thousand words of notes, and giving them detailed analyses and specific advice. And I have studied the presentations of the world's best speakers—including politicians, executives, business leaders, and teachers—to see what I could learn from them. The product of all this observation and experience is contained in this book.

Originally, I was trained to be a teacher. I was taught calculus so I could teach math and guided through Shakespeare so I could teach English. But nobody ever taught me presentation skills—the qualities that make the difference between merely speaking to an audience and actually being able to reach that audience.

After a nightmare teaching experience early in my career, I realized that I wouldn't be successful unless I worked on my presentation and communication skills. I vowed to do that, no matter how much effort it took.

I can't tell you how much I underestimated the work and resources I would need. I spent hours attending workshops, reading books, and even looking back through all of the materials I studied to get my education degrees. But the theories and information I found didn't give me the useful, specific advice I wanted. I decided to change my approach, to go out into the "real world" to see what I could learn. I joined a large software company and I began training trainers, the people who would work with our customers to show them how to use the software we sold.

I soon realized the trainers needed help in the very same areas that had been missing from my studies as a teacher. To get results from your audience— to actually change their behavior—you need to learn such things as how to make your material enticing, overcome your nervousness, inspire confidence and credibility, and even make your presentation entertaining.

I continued to try to seek help in books, but did not get the solutions I wanted. Even if their suggestions were sensible, none told me how to implement them: What I found was only theoretical fluff. I began to work on coming up with my own ideas for meeting the challenges of presenting and how to transfer those skills. My goal was to give people practical and actionable suggestions.

When I began to teach my ideas in my sessions, I started to get fantastic evaluations. So I proposed that the company put into effect a Trainer Education Plan I developed that I thought would help all its trainers get good evaluations. It became one of the company's most successful internal training procedures.

Eventually people wanted to use a similar procedure for other departments. I myself used it to work with many different kinds of employees and even end users, and I varied it to suit people with many different kinds of needs: HR people, technical professionals, project managers, executives, department chairs, financial professionals, sales professionals, physicians, nurses, therapists, pharmacists, and academic faculty. All of them were tremendously enthusiastic about what they learned from my training.

In response to many requests, I became a communications consultant to other companies, educational institutions, and private clients. I developed many programs to deal with specific presentation issues. This comprehensive manual contains key material from all of them.

I have helped thousands of business and academic leaders improve their skills and techniques with great success. This book is a distillation of what I teach them. I am certain that what worked for them will work for you, too.

HOW TO USE THIS BOOK

This book is divided into three parts, all of which are essential to successful presenting:

1. Content Creation
2. Delivery Skills
3. Audience Management Techniques

At the end of every chapter is a section called "Your Turn." It consists of the highlights of the chapter and some exercises that will help you put the ideas into action to create your own presentation, deliver it well, and manage the audience like an expert. Since many of the exercises require your written answers, I recommend that you record them by hand in a notebook set aside for this purpose, or write them on your computer and print them out and keep them in a binder so you can have them accessible for quick reference as you work on putting the principles in this book into practice.

Presenters at any level can use this book. If you are a novice, I suggest you read it from cover to cover, because it gives you all the basic advice you need. Experienced presenters should also read it thoroughly, since I know you will discover here and there throughout the book specific suggestions you can use to make your presentation even better.

If you are neither a beginner nor an expert, you may prefer to start with whichever of the three areas you want to work on first. For example, if you want to know how to start with a killer opener, turn to chapter 5 right now and see for yourself.

I suggest you work on one chapter at a time. This month, for example, concentrate on creating an irresistible menu, next month work on starting with a killer opener, and dedicate the following month to mastering the techniques that will help you command with your body.

With dozens of unique techniques and advice in so many areas, this book will also serve as a complete reference guide that you can turn to for presentation advice throughout your career.

If you're experienced, you might think you can't become even better than you are. But I think it is important to keep what in martial arts is known as the "white-belt mentality"—the ability of masters at the black-belt level to keep the attitude of a white-belt beginner and be open to new ideas. This is what makes them great. The same is true of presenters, and I believe that I can bring you to an even higher level.

If you're a beginner, you may doubt you can become an outstanding speaker. This is simply not true. In this book, I'll help you improve the areas where you need work. But even more important, I'm going to help you identify your strengths and take advantage of them. That's what is really going to make the difference.

There are five stages of learning.

At the first stage you're skeptical: "What is that guy talking about?"

At the second, you're receptive: "I can see what he's doing."

At the third stage, you're engaged: "I can do what he's telling me, with help."

At the fourth stage, you're sold: "I can do it by myself!"

And at the fifth stage, you've mastered it. "I can teach this to others."

I'm going to get you to the fifth stage for your next big presentation.

The fact is, anyone can learn to be a good presenter. Even more exciting, everyone can learn to be a compelling one. I have brought thousands of people on this journey. Now it's your turn.

Part One

CONTENT CREATION

Attract your audience to the presentation with content they won't be able to resist, and keep them there by subtly revealing to them the underlying emotional reasons they should want it. This section will help you create core content that is exactly what your audience wants to hear, put it into a form that makes it easy for you to deliver, and present it in an attractive PowerPoint show.

Chapter One
Prepare an Irresistible Menu
Be certain your audience will crave everything you have to say

Chapter Two
Create Your Core Content
Make it easy for you to deliver and for your audience to follow

Chapter Three
Map Out Your Message
Coordinate what you say and what your audience sees

Chapter Four
Add Power to Your PowerPoint
Make your visuals clearer and more memorable

Chapter One

PREPARE AN IRRESISTIBLE MENU

Be certain your audience will crave everything you have to say

From having consulted hundreds of presenters and viewed thousands of presentations, I see the one critical mistake most presenters make. They focus on what *they* want rather than what the *audience* wants. What every audience wants to know is what's in it for them. But that is only the first step.

You have to make it clear to the audience *why* they would want the items on your agenda. Knowing why creates desire—the motivation to stay in their seats and crave every word you have to say. What's unique about my approach is it gives you an understanding of how to create desire and work with it to compel your audiences to listen and learn.

There are three things you have to do:

- Identify *what* your audience wants—the reasons they would say they're coming to hear you.

- Describe *why* they'd want what you're giving—the subconscious reasons they would be attracted to what you have to say.
- Suggest *how* you're going to give it to them—create a sense of mystery that will lead them into the central core of the presentation.

Identifying what you're going to give people will help you create your agenda, the items I call the *takeaways*. The takeaways appeal to the left part of the brain, the part that handles logic. They represent what's in it for the audience members, the tangible things they will learn.

It's like posting the menu on a restaurant door to lure people in. You can use this "menu" to promote your presentation and attract the audience to come, and you can leave it visible, onscreen when they enter as a further enticement.

However, telling them what you'll give them isn't nearly as important as making sure they know why they would find it valuable. Oddly, when I ask, "Why would your audience want the takeaways that you're offering them?" most presenters don't have a ready answer. *What makes the Rule the Room method unique is that it will help you analyze the emotional needs of your audience and be able to convey to your audience exactly why they would want to hear what you're about to give them.*

To lead into your presentation, suggest how you'll make the learning possible. This appeals to their curiosity and intrigues them with a mystery: How will this speaker deliver on this promise?

Making sure the tools you give them will meet their needs and intriguing them by suggesting how you'll deliver them will make your audience crave what you have to say. But explaining why they would want that content is what will make your presentation irresistible.

Here's how to do it.

Identify What Your Audience Wants

Do your research

Email the audience
To engage your audience members, the theme of your presentation must appear to have value to them and be in line with their goals. It is essential you know what specific topics will be of interest. The best way is to ask them.

If you can get the email addresses of the people who will be attending your presentation, doing your research is as easy as composing an email and clicking Send.

The email can be very brief. People prefer messages that get right to the point. Here's what I wrote when I was preparing a presentation for corporate managers on how to give an effective webcast: "Please tell me the top three things you'd like to know more about giving an effective webcast." You can simply substitute the subject of your presentation for the words "give an effective webcast."

When you look through the replies, you will see certain topics come up over and over again. These are the topics you need to include because they are what people want to learn about. These will serve as the foundation for the takeaways we talk about later in this chapter.

Interview the audience

While the email tells you *what* your audience wants, an interview will reveal *why* your audience wants it. If possible, get this information by actually talking to one or more individuals who are representative of the type of group you're addressing. That is, if you'll be talking to employees about choosing the investments for their retirement funds, ask someone whose employer offers a retirement fund what he or she might want to know about retirement funds. If you're trying to sell a product or a service, ask prospective customers what they would want to know about that product or service. To get at *why* they want what you're going to give them, I've developed a formula. Here are the questions you ask them:

- What are your biggest concerns or worries?
- What are the biggest challenges you have with those areas?
- What are the problems they are causing?
- What's your ideal outcome?
- What would getting that outcome do for you?

The answers you get will be the foundation for the "hooks" that I'll explain later in the chapter. But first, we'll focus on the whats.

Create your takeaways

When I made an analysis of the very best presentations in the world, I noticed a striking similarity among them. Every single one promised to give the audience very specific, practical advice.

When you begin to investigate what your audience members want to know, you are beginning the process of creating presentation magic. You are discovering the areas they really care about, which to them are unsolved mysteries. You have to let them know you're going to solve those mysteries.

For people who come to hear me speak about giving presentations, there are many mysteries to be solved, such as overcoming nervousness and keeping the audience's attention. So I use each one of these as a topic idea. Over the course of the presentation, people will take away solutions to each of these mysteries, so I call each topic a takeaway.

Recently, I worked with a client on creating a presentation to tell small community banks about a new service his company was offering.

Richard showed me his working title: "Leasing—Opportunity or Just a Reaction (Lender's Workshop)." The word "opportunity" sounded good, but I really had no idea what this presentation was about. True, I'm not a banker, but I have learned that if a title is effective, even people outside the field to which it applies may be able to understand what's being offered.

Next I asked him to give me the topics he planned to cover. In *Brain Rules*, author John Medina says research suggests most audiences have only about a ten-minute attention span before they drift, so if you are scheduled to present for sixty minutes, I recommend you leave ten minutes for questions (more about that later) and talk for fifty minutes, covering four to eight topics (allowing between six and thirteen minutes each). In his one-hour presentation, Richard planned to cover five topics.

This is how he described them:

- Can leasing provide solutions to challenges facing community banks?
- Are these risky assets?
- Review the leasing value proposition for your customer.
- Examples of local market opportunity.
- Marketing approaches and discussion points.

The first two topics were questions that could be answered with a yes or a no answer. The last two suggested you'd get a list of items. The middle one had a verb in it that suggested action, but the action was unclear.

It's important to remember that adults all tune in to one radio station: WIIFM, "What's In It For Me?" When you present an agenda, they want to be able to figure out immediately how it will benefit them. Richard's agenda didn't make that clear.

Richard suffered from what Chip Heath and Dan Heath described as "the curse of knowledge" in an article in the *Harvard Business Review* (December 2006): ". . . Once we know something . . . we find it hard to imagine not knowing it. Our knowledge has 'cursed' us. We have difficulty sharing it with others, because we can't readily re-create their state of mind. In the business world, managers and employees, marketers and customers, corporate headquarters and the front line, all rely on ongoing communication but suffer from enormous information imbalances."

As a result, Richard used a lot of terms and concepts that might not be familiar to everyone in his potential audience. While that might make him appear credible and authentic during the presentation, it didn't help convey what they'd get out of coming to his presentation.

What, exactly, was being leased? What were the challenges the leasing solved? What exactly were these risky assets he was referring to? And as for item 3: Would everyone in the audience understand what a value proposition was and how it related to their customers?

Good takeaways inspire your potential audience members to think, *Wow, this presenter really gets me. He knows just what I want to know and says he's going to tell me.* And they're caught up in the mystery. *How is he going to do it?*

Make every takeaway specific

For a takeaway to be meaningful, it has to be *actionable* and *of immediate value.*

To help Richard create his takeaways, I asked him to think about this question for each topic: "What tangible, measurable benefit does this takeaway give to your audience members that they can put into action right away?"—and to answer the questions according to this formula:

- Start with an action verb. The trick to doing this is to mentally insert the words "As a result of my presentation, you will be able to . . ." at the beginning of the phrase.
- Use seven words or less. A string of seven items is the maximum number people can hold in their short-term memory.
- Use familiar words. Avoid what I call cliquespeak—using words or assuming a grasp of concepts people new to or unfamiliar to your field won't understand.

Richard's presentation was basically a sales pitch. He was offering community banks a new service that would help them make money by offering types of loans that they perceived as risky and were outside their area of expertise. His company knew how to structure the loans in a less risky manner, and, in addition, his people would make their expertise available to help the community bankers work with new and existing customers on these loans.

Be brief

Completing the sentence "As a result of my presentation, you will be able to . . ." in seven words or less in simple, familiar language was very challenging for Richard. Brevity often is. Mark Twain once said, "I apologize for writing you a long letter. I didn't have time to write you a short one." Being an expert with "the curse of knowledge" makes your task even harder. It took Richard two hours of brainstorming to come up with the following five topics:

- Expand your loan services.
- Get a supportive partner.
- Mine existing relationships.
- Meet your customers' needs.
- Lower your loan risk.

Organize them in the right order

When possible, try to make the last takeaway the one that is the most important.

Richard pinpointed his future banking clients' largest issue—a lack of expertise. So he strategically placed "Get a supportive partner" at the end of the list. He knew it was the thing they most wanted to hear, and he placed it last to give people real incentive to stay through the whole presentation.

His takeaways in their refined order were:

- Expand your loan services.
- Lower your loan risk.
- Mine existing relationships.
- Meet your customers' needs.
- Get a supportive partner.

Create the title for your presentation

Your title is key. It's the main mystery. It's what motivates your audience to attend your presentation in the first place—an immediately useful, measurable outcome or benefit they will take away from the presentation *as a whole.*

Once you have figured out your takeaways, you have defined exactly what your presentation is about, so you are ready to summarize them in one phrase: the title.

Finding a title for my own purposes was very straightforward—"How to Give an Irresistible Presentation"—since learning how to deliver a successful presentation is the overall benefit people expect to get from hearing me.

In Richard's case, I told him to go through the same process as he did in creating the takeaways, with slight modifications.

- Start with an action verb that follows the phrase "After you have listened to my *entire* presentation, you will be able to . . ."
- Use seven words or fewer. Sometimes you have quite a bit to explain, so I propose the solution people often use for book titles. Start with a short, catchy title, and then use a subtitle.
- Use familiar words.

To complete the phrase "After you have listened to my entire presentation, you will be able to . . . ," here's what Richard came up with: "Increase business with new, low-risk loans." That became his title. The bankers in Richard's audience would know from that title exactly *what* they were going to get from his presentation.

Compare that to his original title: "Leasing—Opportunity or Just a Reaction?"

Describe Why They'd Want What You're Giving

Now comes the unique element of your presentation: when you tell them the *whys*.

The *whats*—the takeaways—offer practical advice that appeals to people's conscious needs. The *whys* meet their subconscious needs. They eliminate or minimize anything that is causing anxiety, frustration, disappointment, or conflict, and they enhance whatever brings them pleasure.

Coming up with the whys to describe what they are seeking from your presentation on the very deepest level is challenging but critical. This is why I suggest you conduct interviews as described earlier in the chapter. While the emails will tell you *what* the audience wants to know, the interviews tell you *why*. This process works across every type of audience and for every type of presentation with any type of goal. Many presenters I have coached have found it almost magically effective.

Identify the pain points and pleasure points

Let me mention again the questions I suggest you ask when interviewing typical audience members.

- What are your biggest concerns or worries?
- What are the biggest challenges you have with those areas?
- What are the problems they are causing?
- What is your ideal outcome?
- What would getting that outcome do for you?

The first three questions reveal what I call the *pain points* of your audience. The last two reveal their *pleasure points*. Your goal is to eliminate the first and enhance the second. You do that by offering three things: happiness, success, and freedom. Those are the three universal goals.

These are some of the ways you arrive at them:

- Satisfaction from your work and approval from employers and clients will bring happiness.
- Reaching goals and getting results are measures of success.

- Removing stress and anxiety and having more time for enjoyment gives you a sense of freedom.

People need a mixture of all three elements.

Think of a businessman who's had huge success (he made lots of money) but isn't happy (he doesn't like what he's doing) and doesn't feel free (he works sixty-hour weeks). Someone who is homeless has freedom (lots of time and no obligations) but no happiness or success. An unemployed musician may get happiness out of playing his instrument, but he has no success or freedom.

Telling people how you will meet their emotional needs—how you will relieve their pain points and enhance their pleasure points—is what makes them crave what you have to say.

Using the combination of an email survey and interviews has been immensely effective for me. Just recently, I was creating a presentation to teach project managers how to give an effective validation session. The company's customers were using a new type of customizable software, and validation sessions were a way of assessing whether the customers were happy with the process or needed more attention from the project manager.

I created my presentation based on emails asking *what* they wanted to learn and based on hour-long interviews with three project managers that revealed *why* they wanted to learn it.

After I delivered the presentation, a project manager in the audience came up to me. "When I was listening to you speak," he said, "I felt as if I were with a psychic who answers my questions before I even have to ask them. How did you know what I was thinking? How did you know exactly what I wanted to hear?"

I knew because I had sought out the information from his peers.

Let me go back to Richard. His presentation offered bankers a way to offer loans that were outside their areas of expertise. These were loans for equipment such as a tractor for a farmer or a printing press for a small company. Richard explained that buying a piece of equipment is like buying a car. The item you purchase begins to depreciate as soon as you take possession of it. To the banks that were unfamiliar with this type of lending, the loans for business equipment seemed very risky. After all, they were making the loan based on equipment of a certain value at a certain amount, but with each succeeding day the value diminished.

Richard's company had figured out a way to structure that type of loan so it could be profitable and also more secure. What's more, his company would provide the expertise to bankers to help them explain and customize the loans for their customers. If he could get the bankers in his audience to see why this would make them happier, successful, and free, I knew he could double or triple the normal attendance at his presentations and have the rapt attention of his audiences. He just needed to put the *whys* into words.

Say how the takeaways relieve pain points and enhance pleasure points

When presenters can't tell me why an audience would want what they are going to present, I ask them this: "How will each of your takeaways relieve the pain points and enhance the pleasure points of your listeners?"

Richard came up with many answers. The pain points included having to turn down customers who wanted loans, working overtime trying to find leads, and worrying about risk. The pleasure points included satisfying existing customers' needs, attracting new customers, being creative about generating new business opportunities, and putting more loans on the books.

Note the change in his perspective by this point. Rather than thinking about what he wanted to convey (or what he *thought* his audience wanted), he was now thinking about his customers' actual emotional needs—*why* they would want what he was telling them.

Define how the takeaways offer happiness, success, and/or freedom

But it's my third question that is the *aha!* moment for most presenters. It certainly was for Richard: "How will each takeaway offer them happiness, success and/or freedom?" Having defined their pain points and pleasure points, he was easily able to determine why the takeaways benefited them.

Takeaway: Expand your loan services. *Why it's beneficial:* "When they make equipment loans, they'll have a new source of income. This will make them happy," he said, "because they will enjoy having more business and feeling more productive. It will bring them success because it will increase their bottom line."

Takeaway: Lower your loan risk. *Why it's beneficial:* "All bankers worry about making loans when there's a high possibility of risk. With these loans they're feeling more confident because they'll understand that depreciation risk isn't going to be a concern."

Takeaway: Mine existing relationships. *Why it's beneficial:* "The bankers will be happy they can go back to existing customers rather than have to depend only on new leads. They'll feel successful because they'll increase their business."

Takeaway: Meet your customers' needs. *Why it's beneficial:* "The bankers will be happy about being able to please their customers, many of whom were small business owners who preferred not to have to look elsewhere for an equipment loan."

Takeaway: Get a supportive partner. *Why it's beneficial:* "The bankers will feel freedom from stress, because my company will provide the expertise and backup to do these complicated loans properly and efficiently. They will also be free of anxiety about making errors or looking foolish, because my people will be alongside them in client meetings to answer any questions."

Richard now had powerfully appealing elements for his presentation. This gave him the basic structure and ensured he'd keep the audience attentive, since as he "solved the mystery" of each topic, he could immediately introduce a new one. When the mysteries and the solutions come regularly, the entire presentation is like a Pavlovian exercise. You keep your subject engaged with periodic rewards, and they remain engaged because they know the entire mystery won't be solved until you get to the end of the presentation.

Suggest How You're Going to Give It to Them

By defining the way you'll relieve their pain points and satisfy their pleasure points, you tell your audience *why* they'd want your presentation. I then asked Richard to form a sentence naming each takeaway (the *what*) that summarized the reason they'd want it (the *whys*) and hinted at the way to achieve it (the *how*). The audience can't resist the bait. That's why I call those suggestions the hooks.

Create your takeaway hooks

What (takeaway): Expand your loan service		
Why	Happiness: more income	+
How	Equipment loans	=
Hook: "I'm going to show you how to make equipment loans a new source of income."		

What (takeaway): Lower your loan risk		
Why	Freedom: fewer concerns about risk	+
How	Structure loans a new way	=
Hook: "I'm going to show you a way to structure these loans so depreciation isn't such a risky concern."		

What (takeaway): Mine existing relationships		
Why	Happiness: satisfy customer Success: get new prospects	+
How	Offer additional types of loans to existing customers	=
Hook: "I'm going to show you how to take customers who had come in for other types of loans and make them into prospects for an additional type of loan."		

What (takeaway): Meet your customer's needs		
Why	Happiness: help small business owners	+
How	Figure out how to finance equipment	=
Hook: "I'm going to show you how to help your customers who are small business owners by providing a loan for equipment they need."		

What (takeaway): Get a supportive partner		
Why	Freedom: no anxiety about needing backup or lacking expertise	+
How	Be mentored in making types of loans that are new to you	=
Hook: "I'm going to show you how I can give you the backup and expertise you need to make a type of loan with which you have no experience."		

See how much more powerful the hooks make the takeaways? Now, the audience members know not only *what* each takeaway is, but also *why* they would want each one, and they are hooked by knowing they'll learn *how* they can make that happen. Richard will introduce each new topic with the hook. And since this happens about once every ten minutes, he'll keep the audience's attention.

(Look at the table of contents for this book and note how it's structured on this premise. Each chapter title represents a takeaway [what you get] and, below it, the italicized line represents the hook [why you'd want it].)

Create your main hook

Once you have the hooks for each takeaway, you can create the main hook for the entire presentation. Just as the main title was a summary of your takeaways, the main hook is a summary of your takeaway hooks. Find it this way.

First, review the takeaway hooks. It might help you to underline the key words that correspond to pain points or pleasure points. Here is what they looked like for Richard:

- Takeaway 1 hook: "I'm going to show you how to make equipment loans a new source of income."
- Takeaway 2 hook: "I'm going to show you a way to structure these loans so depreciation isn't such a risky concern."
- Takeaway 3 hook: "I'm going to show you how to take customers who had come in for other types of loans and make them into prospects for an additional type of loan."
- Takeaway 4 hook: "I'm going to show you how to help your customers who are small business owners by providing a loan for equipment they need."
- Takeaway 5 hook: "I'm going to show you how I can give you the backup and expertise you need to make a type of loan with which you have no experience."

Then summarize them into a main hook. For Richard, it looked like this: "I'm going to offer you a new source of income with less risk plus the expertise you need to expand services to old customers and attract new ones."

When you publicize your presentation to attract people to come, be sure to use both the title (*what* they will learn) and the hook (*why* they would want it and the suggestion of *how* they'll get it). Also list your takeaways.

State the main hook at the very beginning of the presentation, right after you say the title, to remind your audience members what they'll get, reassure them that they'll get it, and make sure they'll stay in their seats until the end of the presentation, to get it all.

Your menu will be irresistible.

Your Turn to Create an Irresistible Menu

Find out exactly what your audience wants and explain it to them so they crave what you have to say.

Review and exercises

Items flagged with arrows require action on your part. If you are uncertain how to proceed, reread the appropriate section in this chapter.

Identify what your audience wants
- ▶ Compose the email you will send out.
- ▶ Create the interview questions you will ask.
- ▶ Create your takeaways (four to eight per hour).*
- ▶ Create your title according to the formula.*

*Start with an action verb, use seven words or less, and use familiar words.

Describe why they'd want what you are going to give them
- ▶ Define how your takeaways relieve pain points and enhance pleasure points.
- ▶ Then define how each takeaway offers happiness, success, and/or freedom.

Suggest how you're going to give it to them
- ▶ Create your takeaway hooks.
- ▶ Create your main hook.

Chapter Two

CREATE YOUR CORE CONTENT

Make it easy for you to deliver and for your audience to follow

Too many presentations are disappointing. The audience members' expectations aren't met, nor do they take anything away.

If you adopt my techniques in putting together your presentation, you will present it comfortably and your audience will comprehend it entirely. This is a secret to making your presentation amazing.

Most presenters believe that getting people to learn is simply a matter of passing along information that they can parrot back. The Rule the Room concept is dramatically different.

I believe that when you have taught something successfully, you will achieve a change in behavior. If you have made your points to the people in your audience and convinced them of your message, they will take action as a result. Once you adopt this mind-changing perspective, you will reexamine every aspect of your presentation, from creating it to marketing it.

In the first chapter, I helped you identify the takeaways you will offer the audience, explain why they will be of value, and deliver the hooks that suggest how you will help your listeners master them. To create the actual presentation, your challenge is to use your expertise to do what you have promised in an exciting and comprehensive way.

When I have one-on-one meetings with new clients who have come to me on their own or whom I have been hired to help with their presentation work, I invariably discover they are very knowledgeable and genuinely enthusiastic about their topics. Yet often, when I observe them in front of an audience, I see all that energy and excitement disappear. The presentation they deliver is not compelling. In fact, they may even bore the audience.

My goal is to help those clients get up in front of an audience and fire it up—to present with the same ease, spontaneity, conviction, and, when appropriate, humor I saw when they were speaking in a more casual, intimate setting.

The first thing I do is tell them to get rid of a conventional script. The number one way to guarantee your presentation will fail is by referring to your notes too often or, even worse, making the catastrophic mistake of reading directly from the script. In general, the more attention a presenter pays to the script, the less attention the audience pays to the presenter.

I have never met a presenter who was not able to talk about the subject of his or her presentation at great length and in great detail in an informal situation. This is why there is no reason to write out, word for word, what you're going to say when you speak to an audience. You're the expert. You know your subject. Trust me, and trust yourself. *You already know what you need to say. You have the words.*

Instead of a script, what you need is a blueprint. Creating this tool will serve two essential purposes.

First, it helps eliminate the primary fear of every presenter: making a mistake with the material. When you create your blueprint, you can be more assured that when you deliver your presentation, you will say everything you had intended and in the right order. Relieving your anxiety on that score will make you feel more secure. Feeling secure will make you seem relaxed. This makes you seem more credible, and as a result the audience will be more receptive to you.

Second, the blueprint helps you ensure that your audience will never be disappointed or bored. It delivers to audience members exactly what they need and what they want—the tools that will enable them to achieve the takeaways that you promised them. This is what will make your presentation different from any other.

To develop your core content, follow three essential principles:

- Define the tasks.
- Solve the mysteries.
- Keep things simple.

Define the Tasks

I have suggested you plan fifty minutes of talk and ten minutes of question time for each one-hour presentation, adjusted accordingly (a ratio of 25:5 in a half an hour, 75:15 for ninety minutes, and so forth). The presentation content should break down as follows: four to eight takeaways of six to thirteen minutes in a one-hour presentation (two to four in a half hour, six to twelve in ninety minutes). Use the takeaways from chapter 1 to build your blueprint.

Step 1: Create the main tasks

Go through the takeaways one by one. Begin by asking yourself, "Does the audience know how to do this?" This is unlikely, of course, since if the audience already knew how to make those takeaways happen, they wouldn't be at your presentation.

For example, when I asked Richard if he felt his audience would understand how to put his takeaway "Mine existing relationships" into practice, he said no. So I told him that he would have to come up with *tasks*—procedures or actions that make the takeaways possible.

You must do the same. I suggest that a presenter come up with about three tasks for each takeaway. You describe the tasks in exactly the same way you described the takeaways.

- Use an action verb.
- Use as few words as possible—ideally, seven words or fewer.
- Use clear and simple language.

When I asked Richard to come up with tasks that would help the audience mine existing relationships, the first one he came up with was "Prioritize your client list." What he would explain and help his audience understand was how to figure out which of their customers were the best prospects for the services Richard was proposing they offer.

Step 2: Create the subtasks

Once you've defined the tasks, go over each one individually and ask yourself if the people in your audience would know how to carry it out. If not, then you have to come up with at least one *subtask*. Go through the same process as in creating the task. Use an action verb, as few words as possible, and clear and simple language.

Looking at his first task, Richard felt the audience wouldn't necessarily know what to do when he said "Prioritize your client list," so he came up with a subtask: "Sort by client type (municipal, agricultural, etc.)." What he meant by this, he would explain to his audience of bankers, was defining which businesses were most likely to use the services his company could help the bankers offer.

Step 3: Create the sub-subtasks

Look at the subtasks one by one, and each time repeat exactly the same process as in step 1. If necessary, create at least one *sub-subtask* in exactly the same manner as you created a task and subtask. Use an action verb, as few words as possible, and clear and simple language.

You may not have to go as far as a sub-subtask. You can stop at any point when you have come up with a directive you know will make your audience think, *Yes. This is actionable. I know how to do it, and I know what to do right now,* provided you give an example.

Richard did in fact go to this level. He thought it would be helpful to give his audience even more particular advice—not only to sort by client type but to go even further and focus on clients who have additional financial relationships. At that point he thought his audience knew very specifically what they had to do once he gave them an example.

Solve the Mysteries

Create the examples

The example is the final level of the task hierarchy. A good presenter gets to it as quickly as possible. It is the most powerful way to ensure that your audience knows how to do what you suggest.

The examples are very important because they're the solutions to the mysteries. If you don't give examples, the next time you give the audience members a mystery, you run the risk that they won't listen, because they won't trust that you have a solution. When you do give them an example, you will see some very active note taking. Your audience members will have been satisfied by getting some actionable information.

Focus on finding and delivering a single example that is so specific and clear that the immediate reaction will be, *Aha! I get it!* If you want to include additional examples, list them in your handout (see chapter 4).

You can use words to describe your example. In some cases, a picture will do a better job, and if you can find one that does, use it. Either way, make sure your audience does not leave the room without a very detailed mental image of how to translate the takeaway you've promised them into an action.

Richard concluded his explanation of how to mine existing relationships by giving his audience two examples of loans he had helped other bankers successfully place. The first was a loan for a piece of farm equipment (Smith Farms), and the second was a loan for a snowplow (Town of Jonesburg). After hearing these real examples, Richard's audience knew how to follow through on the task, subtask, and sub-subtask he had recommended.

Use specifics, not theoretical fluff

One way presenters disappoint an audience is by giving advice that may be sound—a general notion like "build credibility" or even a specific one such as "don't use filler words"—without explaining how to do it. That's what I call theoretical fluff.

The Rule the Room method gives specific practical advice that keeps your audience more attentive and makes them likely to feel that your presentation is worthwhile. The tasks and examples for each takeaway should be *actionable*—*immediately* actionable. Immediacy is important because the longer the gap between hearing an idea and implementing it is, the less of an impression it makes. In no time at all, it can disappear from your consciousness.

I'm not suggesting you can't give the audience sound theory to back up your tasks and examples. For example, in a presentation I do about staying energized as a presenter, I discuss the need for hydration, and at one point the example I give is to drink water. The theory I present in this case is a recent study from the Mayo Clinic that proves that even mild dehydration can drain your energy and make you tired, and that drinking water can flush toxins, carry nutrients, and even nourish the brain.

But the key is to always focus on the real, practical, actionable steps you're giving your audience so they can take what you say and apply it right away.

When they take action—when they make a behavioral change—it's because they have learned something from you. When you cause behavioral change, you will have set yourself apart as a first-rate presenter.

Keep Things Simple

Don't overwhelm your audience with material.

Edit your agenda

- Try to keep your presentation to around five agenda items per hour, ideally ten minutes each but no shorter than six and no longer than thirteen.
- If you discover you have too much content, restructure your presentation—that is, make a single takeaway into two. Cut the amount of content only as a last resort.
- To stay within the guidelines, do not exceed one full page of notes for each takeaway.

Create your own blueprint pages

Use Richard's blueprint as a real-case example to create your own pages. I am going to review the entire process here so you get the big picture. His presentation, as you may recall, had five takeaways:

- Expand your loan services.
- Lower your loan risk.
- Mine existing relationships.
- Meet your customers' needs.
- Get a supportive partner.

For "Mine existing relationships," as I have mentioned, Richard felt his audience would understand the concept but might not know how to put it into practice. So he went to step 1, "Create the main tasks." He used an action verb for each one, described it in fewer than seven words, and used simple language to convey it. I have mentioned one of the tasks he came up with, but he ultimately came up with three:

- Prioritize your client list.
- Find qualified leads.
- Ask the right questions.

He next went to step 2, "Create the subtasks." He considered the first task: "Prioritize your client list." He felt his listeners would not know how to do this without further instruction. So he continued the process. He used an action verb, described it in very few words, and used clear and simple language. He came up with one subtask: "Sort by client type (municipal, commercial, etc.)." Again, he felt his audience would need further instruction. So he continued the process.

For step 3, "Create sub-subtasks," he came up with one. He used an action verb, described it in very few words, and used clear and simple language: "Focus on clients who have additional financial relationships." Would his listeners understand how to do that? He felt the answer was yes. He gave the example of two clients (Smith Farms, Town of Jonesburg) he knew had needed loans for leased equipment.

Once Richard had defined the entire hierarchy of tasks and given the example, people in his audience knew exactly what to do. They could leave his presentation and put his suggestions into action. Because they had learned something actionable, they were able to actually change their behavior.

See his sample blueprint page in Figure 2.1. (I have added the labels "Task," "Subtask," and so on, but these words wouldn't appear on the blueprint he actually uses in his presentation.) He also added a couple of notes—they're marked with asterisks—to remind himself to refer to the handouts he would use as additional tools.

SAMPLE BLUEPRINT PAGE

TAKEAWAY: Mine existing relationships

Task #1: Prioritize your client list
    Subtask: Sort by client type (municipal, agricultural, etc.)
        Sub-subtask: Focus on ones with other financial relationships
            Example: Smith Farms, Towns of Jonesburg

Task # 2: Find qualified leads
    Subtask: Reach out to bank boards and investigate competition
        Sub-subtask: Publicize efforts and do research
        *Provide two key documents on handouts: website promotion and email campaign; supply info regarding data collection
            Example: Show brochures; names of services

Task #3: Ask the right questions
    Subtask: Survey customers to elicit needs
        Sub-subtask: Ask about needs and about level of interest
        *Provide sample survey questions in handouts
            Example: Martin Manufacturing Survey results

Figure 2.1. Sample blueprint page.

Here's why the blueprint page is such a good tool.

- *It keeps you from being dependent on a script.* Richard had to glance at his notes only occasionally. He was able to look at the audience most of the time and convey the impression that he was speaking to each personally.
- *It keeps you organized.* It included all the points he needed to make and it listed them in the right order.
- *It prompts you to include all the material.* The key words for the takeaways and tasks served as a trigger that was all the reminder Richard needed

to talk about each topic for periods that ranged between six and thirteen minutes.

- *It is instructive for the audience.* When Richard had finished speaking, the people in his audience knew precisely what actions to actually go out and do.

Your Turn to Create Your Core Content

Develop the structure that will help you present your material so you can easily stay on track and your audience can easily understand and absorb it.

Review and exercises

Items flagged with arrows require action on your part. If you are uncertain how to proceed, reread the appropriate section in this chapter.

Define the tasks

Start with an action verb, use seven words or fewer, and use familiar words.

▶ Create the main task that will make the takeaway possible.

▶ Create the subtasks.

▶ Create the sub-subtasks (if necessary).

Repeat this process for each takeaway.

Solve the mysteries

▶ Create the example.

▶ Cite the theory (optional).

Repeat this process for each takeaway.

Keep things simple

▶ Edit your agenda.

▶ Limit your takeaways to between four and eight per hour.

▶ Create your own blueprint pages.

▶ Look at the example and make a single page of your own.

Repeat this process for each takeaway.

Chapter Three

MAP OUT
YOUR MESSAGE

Coordinate what you say and what your audience sees

Once you have created your irresistible menu and your tantalizing core content, your next task is to combine your words with slides and create a PowerPoint presentation.

By August 2012, it was estimated that 350 PowerPoint presentations are given each second across the globe. So the mere fact that you're putting on a slide show in connection with your presentation isn't very compelling. Certainly how it looks may set it apart, and I will discuss some techniques for making your graphics look good in chapter 4. But before you decide what kind of visuals you'll use and when you'll use them, you have to think about why you are using them.

In putting together a good presentation, here's the critical point to remember: a PowerPoint slideshow is a visual aid. And that's exactly how it should be used: not as a crutch, but as an aid—something that *adds* to your presentation. Many presenters make a huge mistake here.

Look at Figure 3.1, which I actually saw used in a presentation by an anthropologist. This slide is a word-for-word recapitulation of what the presenter said to his audience. This slide benefited the presenter—he could read his message from the screen and dispense with his reading glasses—but it had no value to the people listening to him. In fact, once they realized what they were reading was exactly what the speaker was saying, their interest in the presentation as a whole quickly diminished. What's interesting about watching someone reading to you? Why do you need to look at a screen if you could close your eyes and hear all the information?

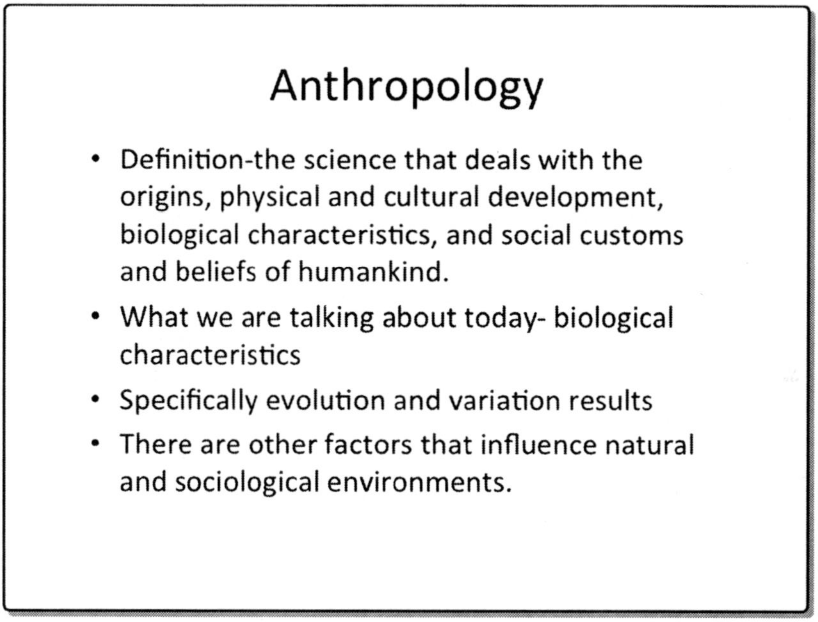

Anthropology

- Definition-the science that deals with the origins, physical and cultural development, biological characteristics, and social customs and beliefs of humankind.
- What we are talking about today- biological characteristics
- Specifically evolution and variation results
- There are other factors that influence natural and sociological environments.

Figure 3.1. A slide like this doesn't benefit the audience.

When you create a slide, make sure it serves a purpose. What you *show* the audience and what you *say* to your audience should work in complementary ways. The idea is to have them work together, so they'll do a better job of putting across your message than either one would alone. I'll show you how to create three categories of slides:

- Opening slides
- Core content slides
- Closing slides

Opening Slides

These assure the audience they're in the right place (because the title is onscreen) and remind them what they're going to hear. You add the rest. This is what continues to hook your audience—when they have to listen to *you* to get the answer to their mystery. There are just two opening slides:

- One *title slide*, which is onscreen when the audience enters the room
- One *main agenda slide*, which lists all your takeaways

Core Content Slides

The highlighted agenda slides serve mostly as placeholders so the audience knows what's about to be discussed. The task slides summarize the main tasks involved in making the takeaway actionable, but you supply the details and describe subtasks and sub-subtasks as necessary. You'll need to prepare:

- Several *highlighted agenda slides,* one for each takeaway. Each of these is identical to the original agenda slide, but the takeaway coming up for discussion is highlighted so the audience members can keep track of where they are in the presentation.
- Several *task slides,* one for each takeaway. Each of these lists the major tasks involved in achieving the takeaway to help the audience follow along as you explain how to make the takeaway immediate and actionable.
- Optional number of *example slides*. These are slides that illustrate an example for a given takeaway.

Closing Slides

There are just two:

- One *summary slide*, the next-to-last slide. It repeats the agenda to remind the audience of what they just got (though the actual brief recap of what they've learned comes from you.)

- One *final slide,* which confirms that the presentation is over. It expresses thanks and gives contact information, and remains onscreen after you have left the stage.

The slides should be used only as signals, guideposts, and placeholders (and occasionally, as you'll see in chapter 4, for giving clarity to a complex idea). For the most part, you want your audience to be focused on you, the presenter, and to understand that the core content will come directly and only from you—because that's what makes them stay attentive.

To see how to coordinate your words and the titles, here's a slide-by-slide description of the PowerPoint show my client created for his presentation to community bankers. I've included some step-by-step explanations that can serve as the template for your own presentation.

On the left side of the page you'll see what the audience sees and why it's there.

On the facing page, you'll see what Richard says. These are his blueprint pages. For each takeaway, there's a single page containing the name of the takeaway and of the associated tasks, subtasks, and, if needed, sub-subtasks, examples, and theories, as well as his notes.

This shows how Richard integrated his visuals with his presentation and is meant to give you an example of what a basic blueprint looks like. I suggest you follow this example, since this same process works for any kind of presentation. Once you have created your blueprint, print a copy and use it as a reference throughout your presentation.

For illustration purposes, I have used plain text on virtually all the slides in this chapter. To enhance your presentation, you will find more details in chapter 4 about choosing and creating strong graphic images, and parts 2 and 3 of the book will explain how to deliver your presentation and manage your audience.

But your presentation preparation starts with a blueprint.

A Sample PowerPoint Presentation

Title slide: What your audience sees

Increase Business With New, Low-Risk Loans

Ideas for Lenders

Before you sit down, please take a handout from the back table

The title slide should be onscreen at least fifteen minutes before the presentation starts. It should have a strong image and convey three pieces of information:

- *The name of your presentation.* It reminds the audience what it has come for.
- *The name of the intended audience.* You want to convey to your audience that this presentation is not generic but intended specifically for them and their needs. Richard's presentation is intended for lenders, so his title includes the words "Ideas for Lenders." If you were presenting to school administrators, you would say "Ideas for School Administrators"; if you were presenting to personal trainers, you would say "Ideas for Personal Trainers"; and so on.
- *A directional to pick up a handout.* I always recommend that you give out handouts (more about that in chapter 4) and give an onscreen prompt to pick them up. The prompt saves you the trouble of handing them out and accustoms the audience to getting directions from you and following through.

Title slide: What you say

(Chapter 5 provides detailed instructions for introducing yourself, presenting your credentials, and conducting the *circle of knowledge* for your own presentation.)

Introduce yourself

Example: "Hi. My name is Richard White."

Give your credentials

Tell the audience how what you do will help them. Example: "I help community bankers find new income sources."

Deliver the main hook

Example: "I'm going to offer you a new source of income with less risk plus the expertise you need to expand services to old customers and attract new ones."

Use the circle of knowledge to elicit requests for your takeaways (optional)

This technique prompts the audience members to say aloud what they want from the presentation and helps stimulate their interest. Example: "Take thirty seconds and write down what you think are the top three qualities of a great loan."

Write down the takeaways on a whiteboard

If you've done your research, the takeaways they want are the ones you're already prepared to discuss. Sure enough, they will appear on the main agenda slide, which follows.

Main agenda slide: What your audience sees

Agenda

- Expand your loan services
- Lower your loan risk
- Mine existing relationships
- Meet your customers' needs
- Get a supportive partner

The main agenda slide is the first time the audience members will get to see exactly what they get for staying and listening to your presentation. It contains only the list of four to eight takeaways for the one-hour presentation you created per the instructions in chapter 1.

If you have a ninety-minute or two-hour presentation, you would list the total number of takeaways (eight to sixteen) on the slide.

Main agenda slide: What you say

Introduce the agenda. Don't read the agenda items to your audience. Give them a moment to read the slide themselves, and then introduce the agenda by summarizing what you'll be doing. That is, mention the number of takeaways you'll be giving them (five, in Richard's case), and paraphrase the goal indicated by the title (which, in Richard's case, is a way for his banker audience to expand their business in a very conservative way). Example: "I'm going to show you five specific strategies to increase loans with less risk."

Highlighted agenda slides: What your audience sees

Agenda

- Expand your loan services
- Lower your loan risk
- **Mine existing relationships**
- Meet your customers' needs
- Get a supportive partner

You will need one of these slides for each of your takeaways.

This slide has exactly the same text as the main agenda slide, except the specific takeaway you are about to discuss is highlighted in bold text in a contrasting color. This makes it clear to audience members what they are about to learn and where you are in the presentation. Pictured above is the highlighted slide for the third agenda item.

Highlighted agenda slides: What you say

As you begin to discuss each takeaway, you introduce the hook, and, where necessary, you should indicate that you are making a transition. For the second takeaway, you might say, "Next, I'm going to show you"; with the third you might say, "Now, I'm going to show you"; and so on. These transition words help people keep their place and suggest that something is about to change— which enhances the mystery.

Deliver the takeaway hook

Example: "Now [you need the transition in this case because this is the third hook] I'm going to show you how to take customers who had come in for other types of loans and make them into prospects for an additional type of loan."

Task slides: What the audience sees

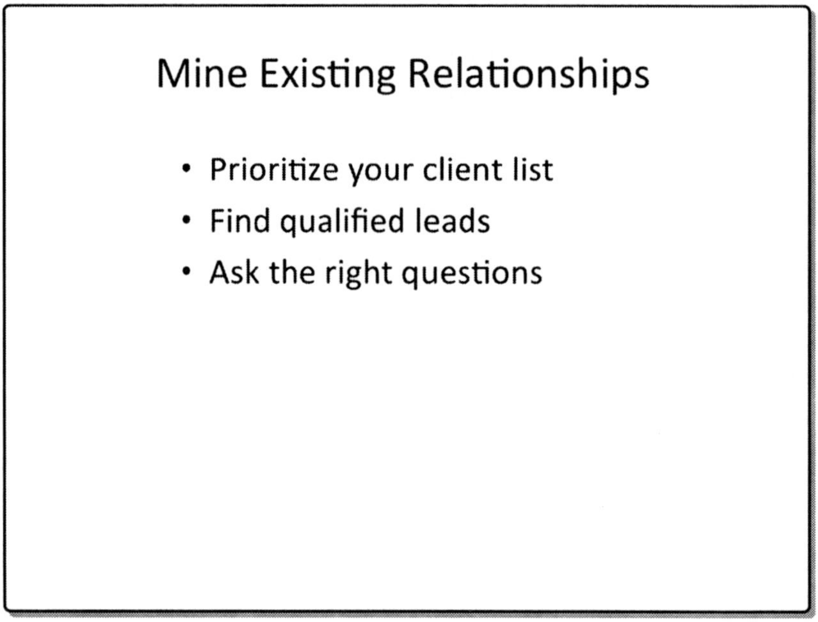

Mine Existing Relationships

- Prioritize your client list
- Find qualified leads
- Ask the right questions

Your discussion of the takeaways and the tasks necessary to implement them is the heart of your presentation. You'll deliver the main portion of your presentation while one or another of the task slides is on the screen.

To keep things simple, the task slide lists only the takeaway and the main tasks required to achieve it. In this example, there are three tasks.

Task slides: What you say

When you discuss each takeaway, you will describe the relevant tasks and any necessary subtasks and sub-subtasks. As needed, also mention research, give examples, and add any notes.

For each takeaway, prepare a single blueprint page like the one I introduced in Figure 2.1 above. Omit the words "takeaway," "task," and so on. Instead, get a quick picture of where you are by using different tab stops (indentations) to show takeaways, tasks, subtasks, and so on, and also use color codes or some other way to distinguish between categories (all caps for takeaways, bolds for tasks, and so on; see below).

Make brief reminder notes (to refer to handouts, to ask for questions, etc.) and use no smaller than a 10-point font so the page is legible. Here's an example of what Richard's takeaway page actually looked like:

MINE EXISTING RELATIONSHIPS   [Takeaway is capped]

Prioritize your client list   [Task is in bold]

   Sort by client type (municipal, agricultural, etc.)   [Subtask is underlined]

     Focus on ones with other financial relationships   [Sub-subtask is in smaller type]

       ***Ex:** Smith Farms, Town of Jonesburg*   [Example is italicized]

Find qualified leads

   Reach out to bank boards and investigate competition

     Publicize efforts and do research

     *Provide two key documents on handouts: [Note to self is asterisked]
website promotion and email campaign;
supply info for data collection

       ***Ex:** Show brochures; names of services*

Ask the right questions

   Survey customers to elicit needs

     Ask about needs and about level of interest

     *Provide sample/survey questions in handouts

       ***Ex:** Martin Manufacturing; Survey results*

Example slides: What the audience sees

You don't always need a picture, but I suggest that you illustrate your example with a slide whenever the slide can enhance what you have to say (see chapter 4).

For the second task, Richard used a picture of one client whose harvest machine he financed and another who bought snowplows, and he discussed how the deal was arranged.

Example slides: What you say

Comment about the slide

Example: Richard says something like, "Take a look at this slide. One of our community banks had clients I'll call Smith Farms and the Town of Jonesburg." He would tell the story of the bank's new capacity to give leasing loans for necessary equipment thanks to his services, strengthening the ties to these clients and creating new business for the bank. Given a specific, immediately actionable example, an audience may take notes at this point; in Richard's case, banker audiences can imagine a client of their own to whom this type of financing would apply.

Repeat the process

After the example, begin the discussion of the next task. Continue until you have covered all the tasks.

If you are going to use an example slide for only one task, consider discussing that task last, so that you can immediately move to the next task slide. But if you will be using slides to illustrate two or more tasks, just return to the task slide in between the two tasks.

If you will be using many slides and want to ensure that your audience can follow, you may want to work with the task slides in the same manner as with the agenda and the takeaways: Prepare a separate slide for each task. The slide has exactly the same text as the task slide, except the specific task you are about to discuss is highlighted in bold text in a contrasting color. This makes it clear to audience members where you are. Note that if you do it this way, your handout will be longer, of course, since the handout should have an image for each slide in your presentation.

Summary slide: What the audience sees

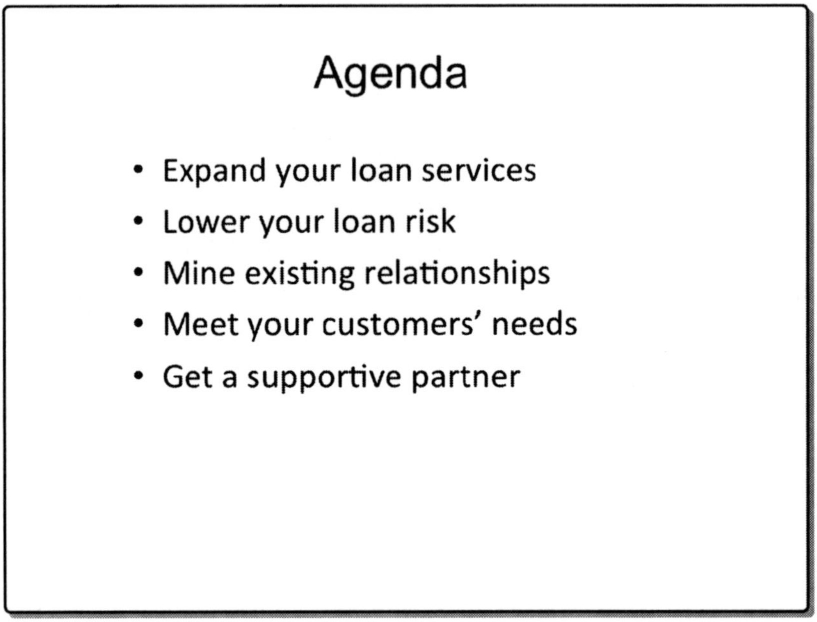

Agenda

- Expand your loan services
- Lower your loan risk
- Mine existing relationships
- Meet your customers' needs
- Get a supportive partner

The summary slide repeats the agenda.

Summary slide: What you say

This is the conclusion of the presentation.

Repeat the introduction

Remind the audience what they got and why they wanted it. Point out to the audience that you have given them immediately actionable information. Example: "You have just learned five strategies to create new sources of income with less risk."

Ask for final questions

Take care of the audience's remaining needs. As always, phrase your request to indicate that you expect questions, and invite questions about any aspect of your presentation. "What questions do you have about [the subject of your presentation]?" Example: "What questions do you have about increasing business with new low-risk loans?"

Final slide: What the audience sees

This is the last thing the audience sees, and it should remain onscreen after you leave the stage. It has two elements: a thank-you (a nice gesture, in addition to your expressed thanks) and contact information.

Final slide: What you say

Offer to stay for individual questions
Example: "It's five o'clock. Those of you who have any additional questions, please stay."

Thank the audience
Thank them for something specific. Example: "Otherwise, thank you for being so attentive."

Add a pleasantry to conclude the presentation
Example: "Have a great day." Making it clear that you have finished prompts the audience to applaud.

Additional Notes

Questions

As I have explained, build in ten minutes of question time per hour—five minutes for questions during the presentation and five minutes at the end. (You may be unaccustomed to getting that many questions, but I will explain how to do this in chapter 14.)

As a rule of thumb, solicit questions at the end of every other takeaway, just before you introduce the next highlighted takeaway. Make a note on your blueprint to remind yourself to ask for questions about points you've just covered (so you can take questions that are directly related). At your first solicitation, at the end of takeaway 2, you would ask, "What are your questions about [takeaway 1] and [takeaway 2]?" That helps ensure that the audience confines the questions to those topics. (More about this in chapters 13 and 14.)

Pace markers

Chapter 13 explains in great detail (under "Document the Timing") how you should manage the timing of your presentation to end on time every time. You should have timed your presentation so you know the approximate time you should be beginning each takeaway. Be sure to note the goal time in the margin of the blueprint you are working from so that if you are running long or short you can use the pacing tips in chapter 13 to compensate.

A Typical Sixty-Minute Timetable

You can see how all the elements of a presentation come together in the complete one-hour timetable laid out on pages 48–49. I used this timetable in preparing one of my own well-received presentations, and I include it here so you can "look under the hood," so to speak.

A good presentation, like any good performance, looks easy, but when you look at the timetable, you can see that getting it right requires a lot of thought. Still, when you analyze what you must do as a step-by-step recipe, the process becomes more clear.

What you say during your presentation can be divided into three categories:

- Seven brief introductory and concluding segments, each part of which lasts just ten seconds. The introductory segments include introducing yourself, giving your credentials, delivering the main hook, and introducing the agenda. The concluding segments include a takeaway summary, an offer to stay for individual questions, and thanks.
- Three interactive segments. The circle of knowledge is about three minutes long, and the two question periods are each a couple of minutes long. During these segments, the audience is doing most of the talking.
- Four to seven takeaway segments of approximately four to eight minutes long. These require the most preparation, because during these you deliver the key information to your audience.

While you're speaking, the audience will be looking at your slides, which will help them follow along. The slides fall into four categories.

- Four basic slides that contain very brief phrases: your title slide, the main agenda slide listing your takeaways, the summary slide (a repeat of the main agenda slide), and the final slide (with a thank you and contact information).
- A highlighted takeaway slide for each takeaway. These are identical to the main agenda slide, but the takeaway under discussion is highlighted.
- A task slide for each takeaway. These require the most preparation.
- Example slides (which are asterisked in the timetable, because they are optional). These are visual illustrations of any examples you want to discuss in some detail.

I suggest you make a timetable for the first presentation or two that you create. After that, you will probably not need to lay out the elements in such detail, as the process will become more intuitive for you.

Slide	What they're seeing	What you're saying	Time this portion	Time this slide	Elapsed time
Title Slide		Introduction, credentials. Deliver main hook	:30		
	Title	Circle of Knowledge	4:20	4:50	4:50
Main Agenda Slide	Complete list of takeaways	Introduce the Agenda	:10	:10	5:00
Highlighted Takeaway #1 Slide	List of takeaways Takeaway #1 highlighted	Deliver takeaway #1 hook	:10	:10	5:10
Task Slide #1	Complete list of tasks for takeaway #1	Discussion of tasks, subtasks, sub-subtasks, theories, examples	7:50	7:50	13:00
Example slide *			2:00	2:00	15:00
Highlighted Takeaway #2 Slide	List of takeaways Takeaway #2 highlighted	Deliver takeaway #2 hook	:10	:10	15:10
Task Slide #2	Complete list of tasks for Takeaway #2	Discussion of tasks, subtasks, sub-subtasks, theories, examples	6:50	6:50	22:00
		Ask for questions #1	2:50		
Highlighted Takeaway #3 Slide	List of takeaways Takeaway #3 highlighted	Deliver takeaway #3 hook	:10	3:00	25:00

Slide	Slide Content	Action	Time	Time	Cumulative
Task Slide #3	Complete list of tasks for takeaway #3	Discussion of tasks, subtasks, sub-subtasks, theories, examples	7:50	7:50	32:50
Highlighted Takeaway #4 Slide	List of takeaways Takeaway #4 highlighted	Deliver takeaway #4 hook	:10	:10	33:00
Task Slide #4	Complete list of tasks for takeaway #4	Discussion of tasks, subtasks, sub-subtasks, theories, examples	8:50	8:50	41:50
Example Slide *			2:00	2:00	43:50
Highlighted Takeaway #5 Slide	Complete list of takeaways, with takeaway #5 highlighted	Ask for questions #2	2:00	2:00	
		Deliver takeaway #5 hook	:10	2:10	46:00
Task Slide #5	Complete list of tasks for takeaway #5	Discussion of tasks, subtasks, sub-subtasks, theories, examples	8:30	8:30	54:30
Summary Slide	Complete list of takeaways	Takeaway summary	:10		
		Ask for final questions	5:00	5:10	59:40
Final Slide	Thank you message; Contact information	Offer to stay for individual questions; Thank audience; Extend a warm wish	:20	:20	60:00

Your Turn to Put the Power in Your PowerPoint

Make sure the slides you use coordinate with and enhance (not repeat) the words you say.

Review and exercises

Items flagged with arrows require action on your part. If you are uncertain how to proceed, reread the appropriate section in this chapter.

Prepare your openers

- ▶ Decide what the audience will see on the title slide.
- ▶ Decide what you will say in relation to the title slide.
- ▶ Decide what the audience will see on the main agenda slide.
- ▶ Decide what you will say in relation to the main agenda slide.

Prepare your core content slides

Use the blueprint pages you created in chapter 2.

- ▶ Decide what the audience will see on the highlighted agenda slide.
- ▶ Decide what you will say in relation to the highlighted agenda slide.
- ▶ Decide what the audience will see on the task slide.
- ▶ Decide what you will say in relation to the task slide.
- ▶ As needed: Prepare your example slides.
- ▶ Decide what the audience will see on the example slide.
- ▶ Decide what you will say in relation to the example slide.

Repeat this process for each takeaway.

Prepare your closing slides

- ▶ Decide what the audience will see on the summary slide.
- ▶ Decide what you will say in relation to the summary slide.
- ▶ Decide what the audience will see on the final slide.
- ▶ Decide what you will say in relation to the final slide.

Chapter Four

ADD POWER TO YOUR POWERPOINT

Make your visuals clearer and more memorable

I disagree with presentation experts who focus on the visuals. That's like saying you buy a Porsche for the paint job. Without the paint the car would still be irresistible because it's impeccably designed, carefully put together, designed to make you comfortable, and capable of getting up to speed instantly. So is your presentation.

Chapters 1–3 gave you the basics for creating your core content. In chapters 5–16, you'll learn how to deliver and manage your presentation. Your presentation would be irresistible with that advice alone.

But just as the paint job on the Porsche is the finishing touch, the same is true of the visuals for your presentation. Take some time to put on the paint:

- Use pictures to add impact.
- Keep your graphics simple.

- Use illustrations to increase comprehension.
- Use handouts to reach every learner.

Use Pictures to Add Impact

There are many sources for pictures on the web. Search "stock photos" and a large number of sites will pop up. Look for up-to-date information about specific sites where you can find images available for a minimal fee or no fee. Read the information and licensing terms carefully. Copyright law governs the use and alteration of images. The words "royalty-free" mean you might pay a flat fee to use the image but you will not have to pay for each copy or use. The words "copyright-free" usually indicate that there is no charge for use and that you may be able to modify the image as you wish.

When you get to a site that seems appropriate, search key words that relate to your topic to find appropriate images. (I'll give you some specific examples for how to do that in this chapter.) Make sure you understand the terms of use that apply to any images that interest you.

Choose realistic images

I generally recommend avoiding abstract images like the ones in Figure 4.1.

Figure 4.1. Instead of abstractions like these, use realistic images.

A slide depicting real people is better for two reasons. First, realistic images are more likely to get an audience emotionally involved. Second, realistic images are more likely to seem authentic. By using an image that seems inauthentic, you risk having the audience subconsciously make the same judgment about your message.

Find the right image for your title slide

With any presentation, the first goal is to find a strong image for your title slide. Since it is the first thing the audience sees, it should be chosen carefully. To explain the process, I'll take as an example the presentation we have already discussed.

Take your lead from the main title and main hook, which suggest to your audience how you'll enhance their pleasure points and resolve their pain points.

The main title of Richard's presentation is "Increase Business with New, Low-Risk Loans," and his main hook is "I'm going to offer you a new source of income with less risk plus the expertise you need to expand services to old customers and attract new ones."

At the websites offering pictures, he began his search by entering key words related to his message, words such as "assets," "growth," "expansion," and "security."

That's how we found the image for his title slide (Figure 4.2).

Figure 4.2. Richard's new title slide with a picture.

Here are the reasons Richard chose this picture:

- It suggests the main hook: the steel balls are attracted to the magnet, indicating growth and expansion.
- It suggests, subtly, the idea of low-risk: the magnet makes a secure bond with the steel balls.
- It leaves enough room for the main presentation title, audience identification (indicating this is directed at an audience of lenders), and the handout directional.

Find an illustration for each task slide

The task slides are the nuts and bolts of your message, and your audience will be looking at them for an extended period of time while you deliver your presentation. These illustrations must also be chosen carefully.

Just as you took the cue for your initial illustration from the main title and main title hook, you now have to take your cues for a picture from the takeaway title and takeaway hook and find ways to illustrate how you'd enhance the audience's pleasure points and relieve their pain points.

Richard searched key words from his takeaways and hooks on websites that offered pictures. Figures 4.3–4.7 show how he illustrated each task slide and the tasks and hooks associated with each takeaway.

Figure 4.3. Takeaway 1.

Takeaway: Expand your loan services. Hook: "I'm going to show you how to make equipment loans a *new source of income*."

The red apple in the middle suggests that after using Richard's services, his potential clients might be able to add a fifth apple (the red one)—a new source of income. It also subtly suggests that the increase might be significant; the new apple represents a 25 percent expansion.

Figure 4.4. Takeaway 2.

Takeaway: Lower your loan risk. Hook: "I'm going to show you a way to structure these loans so depreciation *isn't such a risky concern*."

The down arrow suggests risk will go down, and the group of hands supporting the arrow suggest it will be a result of the teamwork that Richard's company can provide.

Mine Existing Relationships

- Prioritize your client list
- Find qualified leads
- Ask the right questions

Figure 4.5. Takeaway 3.

Takeaway: Mine existing relationships. Hook: "I'm going to show you how to take customers who had come in for other types of loans and make them *into prospects for an additional type of loan.*"

The mining tool suggests Richard is going to give his clients a solid tool they can use to help burrow into and deepen their current relationships to find gold.

Meet Your Customers' Needs

- Take it to the next level
- Respond to customer requests
- Leverage our experience

Figure 4.6. Takeaway 4.

Takeaway: Meet your customers' needs. Hook: "I'm going to show you how to *help your customers* who are small business owners by providing a loan for equipment they need."

The intent is to help customers not only meet customers' needs but exceed expectations. This fuel gauge is a compelling visual that suggests Richard will help the bankers deliver over-the-top performance.

Figure 4.7. Takeaway 5.

Takeaway: Get a supportive partner. Hook: "I'm going to show you how I can give you the *backup and expertise you need* to make a type of loan with which you have no experience.

This is a great metaphor: the suit-wearing individual represents Richard's typical client, and the bunch of extra arms suggest the helping hands Richard's firm can provide with their expertise and backup ability.

Each illustration left sufficient room for the title and met Richard's criteria:

- It suggested the takeaway hook.
- It suggested how pain points would be relieved and pleasure points enhanced.

Illustrate your final slide

The final impression you leave on your audience must be as compelling as the first one, and it also should be illustrative of the main title and the main presentation hook. I suggest you reuse the first image—the one you've carefully chosen to do all those things—on your final slide. Add words of thanks and any other contact information you want to provide (see Figure 4.8).

Figure 4.8. Richard's final slide.

Keep Your Graphics Simple

There is no shortage of books on how to manipulate the text and the visuals on your PowerPoint slides, and I think you may find them useful. Here, I will point out only the essential points to keep in mind and share a few of the techniques I find most useful in making attractive, effective slides.

Make the text legible

- *Use bold, clear, sans serif fonts.* Arial or Helvetica, which are often chosen for public signage, are good choices.
- *Use a large font size.* I recommend at least 24 points.
- *Ensure contrast between your text and the background.* Use a light background behind dark lettering or light type on a dark background. Otherwise, your slides will be impossible to read in a brightly lit room.

- *Use simple tools.* If you aren't adept with graphics or can't include photos for some reason, simply adding borders or a colored background can make plain text more interesting.
- *Avoid clutter and distraction.* See Figure 4.9.

Figure 4.9. Text can't be read if background is too cluttered or contrast isn't great.

Not only is there too much going on visually in Figure 4.9, but also such a complex image may cause people's minds to wander. The illustrations themselves aren't the message; their purpose is to *deliver* the message. Your graphics aren't meant to entertain, inspire, or delight; their sole purpose is to get your point across.

Use basic tools to add interest

Invest some time in learning to use the graphic design tools that come with PowerPoint. The tutorial that comes with the program is helpful. Once you get the hang of it, you can make your graphics significantly better-looking and more memorable.

Look at the before and after shots in Figures 4.10 and 4.11.

Create Your Session

- Create a menu
- Create variety
- Create slides

Figure 4.10. Basic.

Figure 4.11. Enhanced through use of graphic tools.

By mastering just a few of the techniques that PowerPoint offers, you can customize your slides for your presentation.

Use Illustrations to Increase Comprehension

Words alone aren't always the best way to make your point. Illustrations allow you to present a lot of information at once.

Present a big-picture list

Occasionally, the audience needs to see the big picture. For certain learners, it is essential for them to follow along. This is why at trainer boot camp, after I ask the trainers to write down their strengths, I show the slide in Figure 4.12.

What are your strengths?

Show Credibility
- Overcome nervousness
- Show confidence
- Speak well
- Show I am a content expert
- Show I am an expert presenter

Build Rapport
- Be welcoming
- Meet audience needs
- Show that I care
- Get audience to like me
- Make class enjoyable
- Make them comfortable with help

Engage Audience
- Hook audience
- Keep audience attention

Teach all Learners
- Manage the pace of the session
- Make it easy to follow along
- Make it easy to understand
- Determine whether they got it

Answer Questions
- Set expectations
- Listen to audience questions
- Answer in-scope questions
- Punt out-of-scope questions

Figure 4.12. A list of strengths.

Having the comprehensive list for reference helps them to come up with a wide spectrum of possibilities.

Present a chart

I use the chart in Figure 4.13 to demonstrate how to master volume, pace, and inflection. The chart makes the instructions clearer as I model them for the audience.

Desired Effect	Pace	Volume	Inflection
Build enthusiasm and excitement	Even or slightly faster	Up	Up
Stress importance	Slower. Pause at end of sentence	Down	Up
Contrast two ideas or things	Varying	Varying	Up and then down
Reengage the distracted	Varying: slow down/speed up Pause	Up and down	Up and then down
Show urgency	Varying	Varying	Down
Appear credible and knowledgeable	Pause	Moderate, resonant voice	Up and then down

Figure 4.13. This slide shows how to master tone.

Present step-by-step instructions

I ask my audience to read the slide in Figure 4.14 while I demonstrate how to make small talk comfortably.

Make Small Talk Comfortably

Step 1: Exchange names
- "Hi, I'm Jason. What's your name? Nice to meet you Joe."

Step 2: Get them to talk

Ask prompting questions
- "What's your role?"

Ask furthering questions
- "How are things going?"
- "Tell me about that."

Throughout all of the following: Sit if they sit; stand if they stand; maintain 70% eye contact.

Paraphrase
- "Sounds like <xyz>, is that right?"

Step 3: Meet their needs

Explain what you do
- "You know how some people have this problem? Well, I offer this (Great) solution."

Give them a resource
- "There's a great conference coming up in the spring."

Step 4: Close the conversation
- "Nice to meet you Joe. Enjoy the conference."

Figure 4.14. Ways to make small talk with ease.

Make a point more vividly with a graph

Graphs make information easy to grasp very quickly. Prior to doing a presentation to trainers, I surveyed a group to ask if being drained in the classroom was an issue. I presented the results as a graph (Figure 4.15) that dramatically helped motivate my audience to be attentive to my presentation.

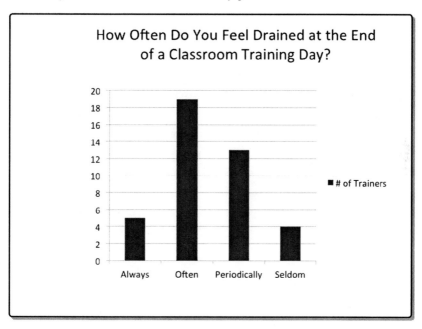

Figure 4.15. Frequency of feeling drained.

I wish I had taken a picture of the audience when I put this slide up. When people saw data they themselves had provided about why the presentation would be valuable to them, even the most disengaged were hooked.

I attribute the enthusiastic response I got at the end of the presentation in part to the effect of this graph.

Use Handouts to Reach Every Learner

Before I began to address one group about giving presentations, I had overheard them debate the value of handouts, so I addressed the topic during my opening. "You may not be convinced of the value of handouts," I said, "but I ask that each of you take one. Within fifteen minutes, at least half of you will be taking copious notes."

At the fifteen-minute mark, I told them to look around. "I had suggested at least half of you would be taking notes by now—and you'll see that's happening."

After this presentation, the debate was over. The company made a policy of preparing a handout for everyone and I believe you should do the same.

Of course, a side benefit of the handout is that you can put your contact information on it. Since a large percentage of your audience will be taking notes on the handout, they will no doubt be taking it home.

I always make available at least one handout per person. Some people need guidelines when they learn; others learn by writing things down. Both of those learning styles—which together will make up at least half of your audience—will benefit from a handout. (More on learning styles in chapter 10.)

Leave the handouts at the back of the room. On your introductory slide, direct people to take them. Watch what happens. People will seat themselves, then look up at the screen and read the message and get back up and go get their handout. You've established a pattern of giving them a direction and having them comply, which helps establish the fact that you will be leading them throughout the presentation.

Keep the format simple

You should have an image of each PowerPoint slide in your presentation. I recommend you stack three of them on the left side of each page and leave room for note taking on the right. You can use two-sided printing so that six slides fit on a single sheet of paper. Figures 4.16 and 4.17 below represent the first two pages of Richard's presentation.

Use the handout only as a supplement

"Your handout helped me listen and take notes. I noticed that it sets up the topics, but it doesn't give me the solutions," said an audience member.

That's the idea. You don't want the audience just to look at your slides or read the handouts. You want to keep the focus on yourself.

Neither the handouts nor the slides offer explanations. However, for the people whose learning style requires taking notes, they're essential, and they help everyone follow along. Best of all, the handouts (like the slides) create mystery. Ideally, your handouts will make your audience members think, *He's going to teach me that? I wonder how.*

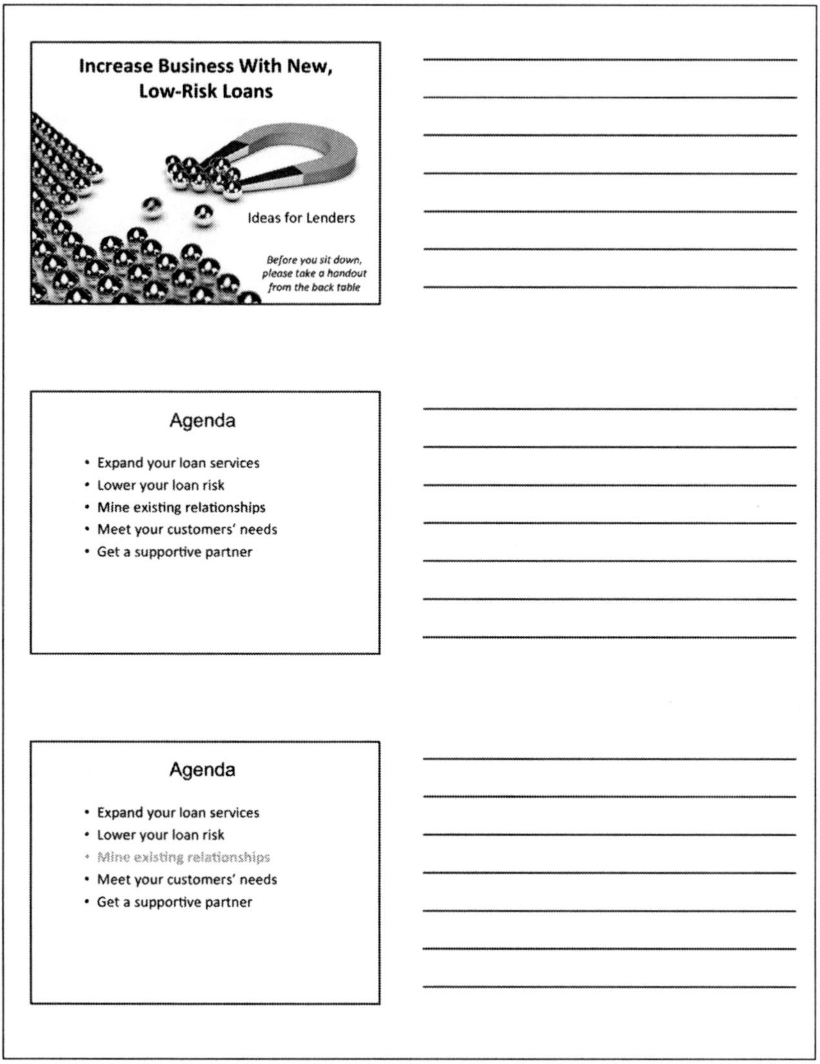

Figure 4.16. Page 1 of Richard's slide show handout.

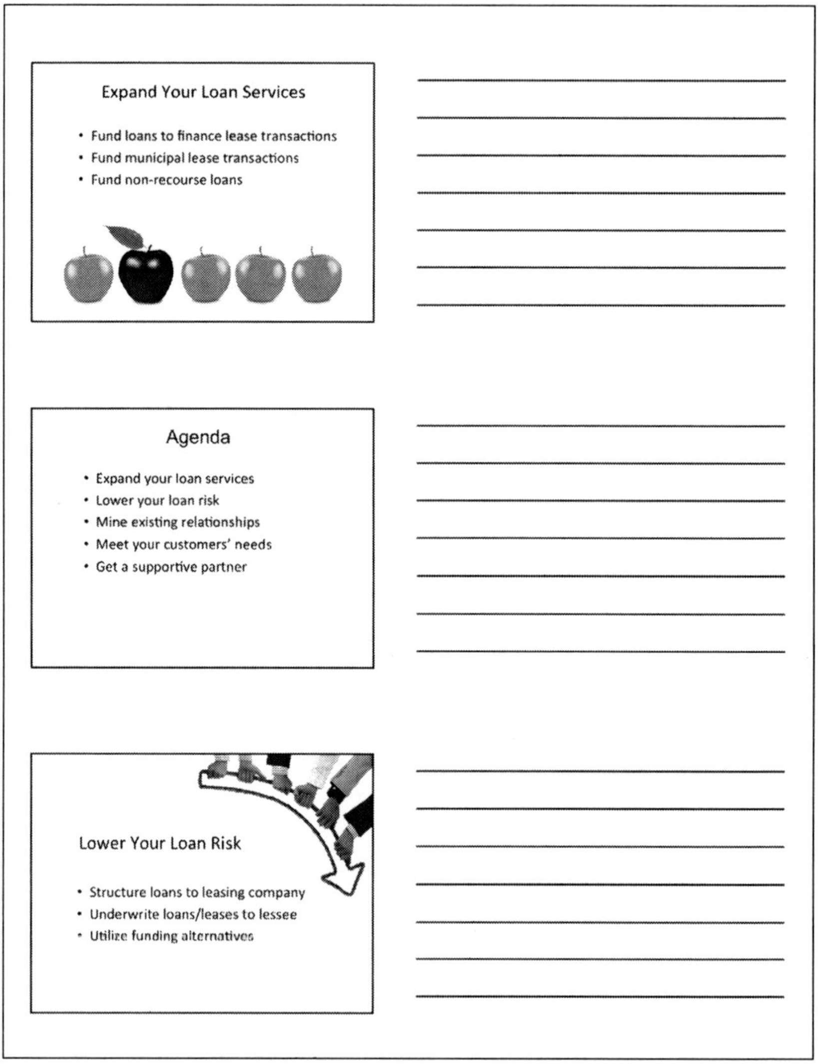

Figure 4.17. Page 2 of Richard's slide show handout.

Your Turn to Add Power to Your PowerPoint

Pictures, graphs, charts, and other visual devices, together with handouts, can help your audience get the big picture and sometimes make a point more efficiently than words.

Review and exercises

Items flagged with arrows require action on your part. If you are uncertain how to proceed, reread the appropriate section in this chapter.

Use pictures to add impact

▶ Find the right image for your title slide. Choose key words you will use to search.

▶ Find an illustration for each task slide. Choose key words you will use to search.

▶ Prepare your final slide.

Keep your graphics simple

▶ Check to be sure the text is legible on all your slides.

▶ Decide what you can do to add interest with basic tools.

Use diagrams to increase comprehension

▶ Look over your presentation and decide where you can use slides to do any of the following:

- Present a large amount of information.
- Present complex information.
- Present step-by-step instructions.
- Present any information more vividly.
- Present information with graphs or charts.

Use Handouts to Reach Every Learner

▶ Prepare your handouts.

Part Two

DELIVERY SKILLS

Creating an immediate and powerful impression on your audience is a matter of standing in the right place and working the room with your body, your words, and your voice. Learn the techniques that will make you project calm and confidence under any circumstances.

Chapter Five

Start with a Killer Opener

Captivate your audience within the first five minutes

Chapter Six

Command with Your Body

Use your face and your body language with dynamic effect

Chapter Seven

Convince with Your Voice

Persuade your audience with the words you choose and the way you sound

Chapter Eight

Overcome Your Presentation Fears

Stay calm and in control in front of every audience

Chapter Nine

Appear Confident and Credible

Show audience members they can trust what you say

Chapter Five

START WITH A
KILLER OPENER

Captivate your audience within the first five minutes

If you tell me you have a panic attack the moment you stand in front of your audience, I'll bet I know what your problem is. And—though all these things matter—it's not because of how you're standing or that your voice is cracking or that you're talking too loud or too fast or that you're sweating. It's not because of anything you *are* doing. It's what you *are not* doing.

You haven't kept your focus. You've forgotten that the presentation isn't about you; it's about your audience. When you're meeting the audience members for the first time, when you're making that first impression, how *you're* feeling and what *you're* doing doesn't matter as much as how *they're* doing and how *they're* feeling. You should be concentrating on *their* feelings and *their* needs.

Everyone wants to know how to get up in front of an audience and connect with it—right away. I will tell you how. Using the Rule the Room principles, you will get an immediate response that will be unlike any you have experienced.

71

The rustling will stop. People will come to attention. Eyes will be fixed on you. That's because you will be using techniques most presenters have no idea about but that will win over even the toughest audience. You may even be surprised to find you're enjoying yourself.

It's a three-step process:

- Get them to trust you.
- Get them to believe you.
- Get them to listen to you.

Get Them to Trust You

The primary need of your audience is to feel safe with you and among their peers, so that's what you must deal with first. Once they trust you, they will feel safe. The best way to start is with a thoroughly rehearsed strong opening.

I suggest you run through your entire presentation at least three times in real time and in the exact circumstances of your presentation. For example, if you're not in the actual presentation room, practice in a room of similar size; if you'll be on stage, practice on a stage. If you are at all nervous, run through the opening portion—the steps covered in this chapter, everything up to the reveal of the topics—at least six times.

I am amazed so many people take such care with the content of their presentation and don't spend much time thinking about the first impression they make when they come onstage.

Some presenters even start by fiddling with the mic. The audience doesn't know if the person on stage is the presenter or the AV tech until the person says, "I guess I'd better turn the mic up. I have a very soft voice."

But these openers, all of which I have actually heard, aren't any better:

- "Can everybody hear me?"
- "I'll talk for about forty-five minutes or so."
- "I know you're all very busy."
- "I'm very glad to be here."
- "I'm a graphic designer."
- "All right, I just want to start with a little story . . ."
- "Hey. So, first and foremost, I really want to, um, thank everybody."

- "Probably the first thing I should tell you is . . ."
- "You guys are awesome."
- "Uh, all right, before I get started . . ."
- "So, I have been up here a few times today, although I have not properly introduced myself."
- "All right, let's get started."

Such awkward comments are not compelling and don't make a presenter seem credible. The audience feels disappointed; its expectations are deflated.

To connect with your audience, even before you say a word, you have to make an impressive physical impression.

Position yourself in the sweet spot

When you come onto the stage, hold your head high and focus on a spot slightly above the heads of the audience rather than making eye contact. At this point, you don't want to be distracted by anyone who might be wearing a hostile or irritated expression.

Walk to the sweet spot, the spot in which everyone in the room will feel as if you are addressing him or her directly. While the exact location of the sweet spot will be different depending on the dimensions of the room, you can use the same technique to find it whether you're in a conference room with an audience of thirty or on a stage in front of a crowd of ten thousand.

Draw an imaginary line right down the middle of the room from your nose to the rear wall, and straddle that line exactly. I highly recommend you check out the room before the presentation so you know exactly where the sweet spot is located and can go right to it.

Find the right distance

The most effective distance for giving a presentation is between five and ten feet from the first row. If you're less than five feet away, people will feel their personal space has been invaded. If you're back more than ten feet, people will feel disconnected or, even worse, that you want to keep your distance.

After reading audience feedback on thousands of presentations, I've discovered many people are very conscious of where the presenter stands in relationship to them and are very forthright in mentioning it. If the speaker stands closer than five feet, they say things like, "You were too close," or even, "You made me really self-conscious and nervous." If the speaker stands too far back, they say, "I didn't feel as if you cared about us." Though the impact on your audience may be subconscious, it is very real.

You don't need to bring along a tape measure to find the right distance. Just use your feet as a gauge. Go approximately five footsteps away from the chairs in the first row for a small group and ten in a larger one.

Assume the right stance

Stand with your feet slightly apart, weight evenly balanced, and arms at your sides. Keep your arms at your sides unless you will be using your hands for a specific purpose. In general, avoid purposeless movement.

Researchers have discovered that the direction in which someone's feet are pointed indicates to whom that person is relating. Check it out: If you observe three people in a group, and one is speaking, look at the speaker's feet. Even if the person seems to be talking to both of the others, if his or her feet are pointing toward only one of them, that's the one with whom the speaker is really communicating.

Ensure that all the people in the room feel included and as if you are talking to each of them by positioning your feet correctly. Draw an imaginary line from the tips of your feet out toward the audience in a triangle shape. Back up if necessary until the angles of the triangle are wide enough to include everyone in the room, but take care not to move too far from your audience.

Some women have told me that they find that stance too aggressive, so I have suggested an alternative version that they may find more comfortable. (Female newscasters often use this stance.) Put one foot in front of the other, front foot facing forward and turned slightly in one direction, back foot turned out slightly as well. (You create the V-spot in this way.) Keep the weight on the back foot. Instead of standing with arms at your sides, you may feel you seem more approachable with your hands loosely clasped in front of your abdomen. (Don't intertwine your fingers, or you may appear to be tensely gripping your hands together.)

Once you're properly positioned, begin to make eye contact.

Make eye contact

If you have a small audience

I define a small audience as any group of thirty-two or fewer. Thirty-two is the maximum size that typically fits into a small presentation room. With a group that size, you should make eye contact with each person in the audience for about half a second per minute.

Train yourself to look at three people every time you pause to take a breath of air (usually every ten to fifteen words). You can start with the people who initially catch your eye, people who seem to be enjoying the presentation, since that will make you less nervous. But as soon as possible, try to look at the ones with whom you are less comfortable making eye contact.

Remember, it's not about you; it's about your audience members. Eye contact makes them feel good, and that will start to show on their faces.

If you have a larger audience

Once you have an audience of thirty-two or more, it becomes nearly impossible to make eye contact with each individual. Instead, mentally divide the audience into nine sections: left, middle, and right, and then front, middle, and back. Look at each of the nine sections for approximately three seconds per minute.

When you appear before a group of fewer than fifty, every person is close enough to detect the movement of your eyes, but that's not the case when you appear before larger groups. You can look at each of the nine sections less frequently than you would look at a particular area in a smaller group, but you must hold your gaze for a little longer so they can see you gaze at their section of the room.

Introduce yourself

Once you have positioned yourself and begun to make eye contact, speak. The audience members want to know who you are, so tell them. Say your full name, because that sounds more professional, and eliminate all the fillers: "Hello, I'm Jason Teteak," "Good afternoon, I'm Jason Teteak," or simply, "I'm Jason Teteak," rather than "Hi, and, um, I'm Jason Teteak," or "All right, I'm Jason."

Speak in a confident voice—that is, keeping your pitch even on every syllable and then dropping it on the last.

If you're speaking to a small group of people who already know you, substitute something simple, direct, and brief as your introduction, such as, "Good morning. Welcome to the August staff meeting."

Give your credentials

Giving your credentials can be very powerful in winning trust if you do it in the proper way. Most presenters think the audience wants to know what the presenter does. But telling your audience what your specialty is and how long you've been doing it isn't going to help you win the trust of your audience members. Again: it's about them, not about you. What will make them feel safe and trusting is hearing how what you do will help *them*.

I asked a new client how he normally introduces himself. "I am a software developer," he began. "I have worked at my company for ten years, and I write code." Then he started to list his achievements.

"Stop," I interrupted. "Just tell me how what you do helps people. What kind of problems do you solve?"

"Interfaces are often difficult. I create interfaces that are easier to use," he said.

"*That's* what you tell your audience," I explained. "What they want to hear—what *every* audience wants to hear—is 'What can you do for me?'" They need to know who you are and why you're the best person to deliver this presentation, but your goal in presenting your credentials is not to promote yourself but to indicate what you have to offer them.

The best way to do that is with an elevator pitch, a summary—short enough to deliver in the course of an elevator ride—that tells people what problems you can solve and what benefits you provide. For example, I could tell my audiences I'm a communication coach for top-level executives and a presentation expert. I could add how many years of experience I have and in how many areas, or I could mention how many thousands of people I've trained or list the names of clients who've consulted with me.

But rather than saying, "I've been teaching people how to do presentations for fifteen years and I've been successful working with thousands of presenters," I explain how I have value to the listener. This would vary depending on the specific topic of the presentation. So I might say, "I help people overcome their fears and actually enjoy delivering their presentations," "I make successful communication simple," or "I help professionals deliver a compelling message."

When I asked my client Richard, the banker, what he considered his clients' biggest problems, he said it was thinking of ways to expand their businesses. Now his credential statement is "I help community bankers find new income sources."

Similarly, rather than saying, "I'm a computer software engineer with twenty years of experience," my engineer client learned to say, "I create software that's easy to use." This works for any profession. "I'm a tour guide who's been living in Paris for a decade" is less appealing than "I help guide others to the trip of a lifetime when they visit Paris."

Think about how your experience will relieve a pain point or enhance a pleasure point to describe your own credentials (see chapter 1 to review the process). Once you do that, your audience will start to feel safe and trust you enough to keep listening, and you can move to the next step.

Get Them to Believe You

When you have their trust, your audience is ready to believe you. Actually, the audience *wants* to believe a presenter. Audience members want to know they've come to this presentation for a good purpose. The way you inspire belief is with the hook you created in chapter 1.

When you deliver the hook, stay still. Don't move your feet, and keep your hands at your sides or loosely clasped in front of you. Your pace should be slower than normal, because slowness implies what you're going to say is extremely important—so important that they need time for it to sink in.

Start with a confident phrase

Instead of a tentative "I hope to tell you" or "Today we're going to cover," use something like this:

- I'm going to show you . . .
- I'm going to tell you . . .
- You're about to learn . . .

You want your listeners to associate the desirable hook with you and realize that they must to be attentive to you in order to get the information they need.

Tell them why they want to listen

As I discussed in chapter 1, the items on your agenda are what your audience wants to know. But the hook tells them why they want to know it—the underlying emotional issues that you determine through your research. After they've revealed their pain points and pleasure points, you figure out how to relieve the first and enhance the second by offering agenda items that will give them some combination of happiness, success, and freedom.

For example:

- If you're presenting to sales professionals: "I'm going to show you how to get your prospect's attention, put your message across, and close the deal."
- If you're presenting to a group of academic administrators: "I'm going to show you how you can get everyone to feel heard in a limited amount of time with a plan of action before the meeting is over."
- If you're presenting to software developers: "I'm going to show you how to test faster and find bugs sooner without a complicated change in your operations."
- If you're presenting to venture capitalists to get funding for your start-up: "I'm going to show you how investing in my company will provide you greater financial rewards in a better market with less risk."

The right hook tells your audience members *why* they should listen to you. It suggests the ways in which they'll be happier, more successful, and/or free. Once you've tapped these emotions in a truthful, compelling way, your audience will begin to believe you and they'll be captivated.

Engaged by the hook, the audience members begin to think, *What are you going to give me? I want to see it!* They crave the takeaways. Now, heighten the anticipation by asking the audience members themselves to come up with the topics that most concern them and demonstrate your credibility by letting them know that's exactly what you will be talking about.

Make all that happen with a unique technique I developed: the *circle of knowledge.*

Get Them to Listen to You

The *circle of knowledge* is a way to get the audience members to reveal what they actually want to know from you and to look good while they do it—and ultimately, it will be a tool to get them to listen.

The simple, three-step process is an unparalleled tool to help you connect with your audience and get them to want to listen to you.

Step 1: Ask a question

Begin by saying, "Before we get started, I want to know what *you* think." Ask them what they think are the top three things that represent a success in the topic you're presenting about. Then, give them thirty seconds to write down their individual answers. Asking the right question is key. For example:

- If you're presenting to sales professionals: "What are the top three qualities you think successful salespeople all have?"
- If you're presenting to a group of academic administrators: "What are the top three things that make an effective staff meeting?"
- If you're presenting to software developers: "What are the top three features that make a new software program appealing to any market?"
- If you're presenting to venture capitalists to get funding for your start-up: "What are the top three criteria a great investment should meet?"

What the question achieves: When I described the *circle of knowledge*, Richard White, who wanted to sell his services to community bankers, wanted to ask, "What are the top three concerns community bankers have?" For a presentation I would make, I would like to ask, "What are the top three areas you need to improve as a presenter?" so I could address those concerns.

But it is pointless to ask a question designed to uncover pain points. Why? Because you won't get many responses. People don't want to reveal their weaknesses publicly. However, if you ask what are the top qualities or skills or results they'd like to achieve in their area, you will get lots of answers. Though they may be unwilling to express their deficiencies, people always know how to state positive goals.

Richard reworded his question to ask, "What do you think are the top three qualities of a great loan?" As a presenter myself, I would ask, "What are the top three qualities that make an amazing presenter?" By making our audience members feel like experts and keeping the topic positive, we gain insights and build our credibility to our audiences.

Spend time on coming up with questions for the *circle of knowledge* that will prompt useful responses. Ask a question that:

- Directly relates to the overall topic of the presentation
- Is expressed in a positive way
- Is open-ended, with multiple right answers
- Is designed to tell you what your listeners want to know about the topic
- Allows the audience to demonstrate some expertise about the topic

Step 2: Request agreement

Ask audience members to take another thirty seconds to discuss and then agree with the person sitting next to them on the best answer.

What this process achieves: Your audience is always a bit apprehensive at the beginning, both about you and about interacting with others. But your question will allow audience members to express their opinions about a topic they care about and to come to an agreement—people love to agree—with a colleague or peer. This makes them loosen up, which makes them feel safer, which makes them more comfortable and ready to enjoy your presentation.

Step 3: Call on a relayer

Ask each pair to assign one of them to be the relayer who states what they came up with.

What this achieves: Using a relayer system will be far more productive than asking for individual responses. People are less hesitant to speak in front of an audience if they are speaking on behalf of someone else, because they don't have to take individual responsibility if their answer is not well received.

In this case, since the question is based on their expertise, people often are eager to answer, hoping to look good in front of and be validated by you and by their peers.

After a minute has elapsed (thirty seconds to write things down, thirty seconds to consult with the relayer), ask, "Relayers, what did you come up with?" They may not be sure whether to raise their hand or not, so I encourage them to be a bit informal by saying, "Shout it out. What are the top three things that make an effective [your topic]?"

As they shout out answers, write them down on a board or a large sticky note if you can. (You'll want to refer back to these later in your presentation to show you've met their needs). When you use the *circle of knowledge*, the answers come so quickly you may have trouble writing fast enough to get them all down. In the hundreds of times I've used the *circle of knowledge*, it has never failed to get an enthusiastic and helpful response.

The *circle of knowledge* is effective and powerful.

- It enlivens the presentation.
- It gives your audience a chance to show its expertise and feel comfortable with you.
- It shows your empathy: You care what they have to say and you're listening to them.
- It tells you exactly what they want to know. To the question of what makes a great loan, Richard's audience mentioned such topics as minimizing risk, using existing customer relationships, and satisfying their customers. Among the qualities my audiences have said will make you amazing as a presenter are showing confidence, looking knowledgeable, using humor, appearing calm and flexible, building rapport, and so on.
- These answers reconfirmed the topics research told us were of interest, but with the *circle of knowledge*, the audience was hearing the answers aloud.
- If people add a topic you hadn't prepared for, but you're knowledgeable in that area, you may be able to weave the topic into your presentation in real time. (I'll make some suggestions for doing that later in chapter 12.)
- At the very least, you've got some market research for the future.
- Best of all, you'll have the perfect segue from what they want to the takeaways that you have. Once you bridge that gap, you will have them exactly where you want them, hanging on every word you are about to say.

Reveal your takeaways

To introduce your main agenda slide, you say, "Here's what I'm going to show you today."

Click on the main agenda slide and let them read your takeaways. Your audience members will discover that what they want and what you're going to show them are nearly one and the same.

Don't read to them. They're adults.

Make your summary

After a couple of seconds, give the actual number of new strategies and techniques they will get and restate the title of the presentation.

For example, when Richard shows his takeaways, he says, "I'm going to show you five specific strategies to increase loans with less risk." When I show my takeaways, I say, "I'm going to show you eighteen new techniques that will help you deliver an amazing presentation."

At this point, they trust you, they believe you, and now they want to listen to you because you've introduced the topics your research revealed they cared about.

Within five minutes you've accomplished all of the following:

- Established your credibility (with your introduction and credential statement)
- Reminded them why they have come (with the topic hook)
- Engaged them in the process and acknowledged their expertise (with the *circle of knowledge*)
- Reassured them you'll give them something amazing (by revealing your agenda)
- Piqued their interest with a mystery (because they're wondering how you'll give them the answers)

They're hooked.

Your Turn to Start with a Killer Opener

The first impression you make is critical. Knowing exactly what you are going to say and do will help you do it best. Concentrating on meeting the needs of the audience will reduce your anxiety.

Review and exercises

Items flagged with arrows require action on your part. If you are uncertain how to proceed, reread the appropriate section in this chapter.

Get them to trust you

▶ Write, in your own words, what you need to remember about positioning yourself for your presentation by answering these questions:
- What is key to finding the sweet spot?
- How do you find the right distance from your audience?
- What constitutes the right stance?
- What should you do about making eye contact?

▶ Decide how you will introduce yourself.

▶ Decide how you will give your credentials.

Get them to believe you

▶ Decide what confident phrase you will start with.

▶ Decide on a hook that will convince people to listen.

Get them to listen to you

▶ Introduce the *circle of knowledge.*

▶ Decide what questions you will ask for the *circle of knowledge.*

▶ Decide how you will request agreement.

▶ Decide how you will call on a relayer.

▶ Reveal your takeaways.

▶ Decide how you introduce your agenda.

▶ Decide what you will say in your summary.

▶ Practice this as many times as you need to feel comfortable, but at least three times in real time. It is ideal to practice in the actual room in which you will be presenting or one similar to it (refer to chapter 8 for additional suggestions). On the day of your presentation, get to the presentation site with time to spare, so you can practice more.

Chapter Six

COMMAND WITH YOUR BODY

Use your face and your body language with dynamic effect

A very effective CEO once told me that if any of her people are having a problem with a client, she knows exactly what to do. She puts that person on a plane and sends him or her off to work things out in person. This is far more effective than a phone conference and many, many times more helpful than writing a memo or sending an email, she says. Nothing compares to a face-to-face meeting.

She intuitively came to the conclusion that my observations have verified and communications researcher Dr. Albert Mehrabian has even tried to quantify—that words are less important than your voice in affecting the feelings and attitudes of your audience, and, even added together, they don't make as big an impression as nonverbal and nonvocal cues.

While there are no reliable, exact measures as yet, from all the anecdotal evidence I have accumulated from my years of doing and observing presentations, I have no doubt that facial expressions and body language play a major role in whatever impression you make on your audience.

Whether you are meeting someone one-on-one or speaking to an audience of five thousand, before you've said a word, people have made some kind of judgment about you. And while your superficial appearance is important—what you're wearing, how fit and groomed you are, and how attractive you may be—they determine what kind of a person you are based on cues that are far more subtle.

Unaware of this, many presenters focus exclusively on the words of their presentation and ignore all the other more important components. They give no thought to the best place to stand when talking to an audience. They don't know how to use their hands or their eyes to give their message maximum impact. When you know how to use the tools of body language and facial expression to enhance your persuasive powers, you will be a far more effective presenter than you ever imagined.

To master nonverbal communication skills:

- Take a strong stance.
- Move purposefully.
- Master eye contact.

Take a Strong Stance

Address your audience at eye level
Being up on stage and looking down at your listeners automatically creates a distance between you and them, a sense that *I'm above you*. Whenever possible, stand at the same level as your audience.

Keep the sweet spot as your default
Ideally, you should stand in the central position I described in chapter 5 as the sweet spot. That is where the audience will find it easiest to relate to you.

Whenever possible, go into the room where you will be speaking before the audience comes in and find the sweet spot so you can walk directly to it the first time you appear in front of them. Review the instructions for stance in chapter 5.

With few exceptions, which I'll mention later in this chapter, stay in that spot the entire time you are speaking. Even if you have to move away briefly, return to it.

Sometimes people have a hard time believing that staying in the sweet spot is going to be effective. "Won't you bore people?" they ask. "Won't you lose their attention?" Sometimes they ask me this in the middle of my presentations.

"How long have I been teaching you?" I ask.

"Two hours, so far."

"Have I kept your attention?"

When the person confirms I have, I explain that part of the reason is that, even though I've talked almost nonstop, I've been talking from the sweet spot.

The sweet spot is where your audience wants you to be. When you stand there, they feel most connected to you.

Overcome barriers

When you are behind a podium, you can't use body language as effectively. It is always preferable to use a lapel microphone and move to the center of the stage rather than to stand behind a podium.

When you're doing a PowerPoint presentation to an audience that is seated at a rectangular or oval conference table, stand about five feet from the closest person and position yourself to the left of the PowerPoint screen from the audience's point of view. (That's because people read from left to right, so they'll look at you and their eyes will continue in the left-to-right direction across the screen.)

If you're seated at the table with your audience, it's unlikely you'll be doing a PowerPoint presentation. In that case, the best spot for you is one that allows you to make eye contact with everyone in the room: in the center of either short end of the table.

Since your feet can't be seen if you're behind a podium or table, use your shoulders to include the audience. Imagine there's a camera perched on each of your shoulders and position yourself so everyone in the room is included in the camera viewfinder.

Move Purposefully

People sometimes think the way to be a dynamic speaker is to use a lot of motion, so they pace around and move their hands all the time. Random movement is just a meaningless crutch. It also distracts your audience.

Use the power of stillness

Keep your body still by default while you are presenting. Great comedians—who generally perform solo, so they can stand anywhere—always stand in the middle of the stage. They never leave the sweet spot, and they keep you focused on them the whole time. The fact that they are not moving is what inspires credibility and demonstrates confidence.

When you practice delivering your presentation in front of an empty room, you should also practice standing still the whole time. Once you severely restrict your movements, any movement becomes more powerful. I know some people are more kinetic than others, and although they're willing to stand in the sweet spot, they just can't resist moving around more than I recommend. I'm not suggesting you never move in a presentation, but I do recommend you keep your feet still until you have a reason to move.

Movement without purpose is called fidgeting, and it is likely to undermine your credibility. To keep your feet still, imagine they are magnetized or glued to the floor and you cannot move them off the ground. Keep your weight evenly distributed rather than leaning any one direction. Imagine that all the people in the room can get their oxygen only from wherever you put your weight. In other words, if you lean mostly to your right, the left side of the room can't breathe, and vice versa. This is a good trick to help you stay centered.

We'll talk more about effective movement in chapter 9.

Move from the sweet spot only when necessary

It is appropriate to leave the sweet spot for these reasons:

- If you want to make an important point, and the movement will help you do so.
- If you need to turn around and walk toward your overhead screen to point something out.
- If you need to move back to the lectern.
- If you need to move toward your audience to demonstrate something. If, for example, you wanted to model something with your audience, you might kneel down in front of somebody and talk to him or her in front of everyone else.
- If somebody asks a question, you might take one step toward that person to indicate you want to hear what is being asked (though you

don't want to get too close, because, if you do, the others in the room may think your topic might apply only to the person you're connecting with and not to them).

- If you're using a visual aid on a board or writing on a screen or demonstrating something. When you're finished with your demonstration, move back to the sweet spot.

Use your hands only to give direction or emphasis
Presenters sometimes put their hands into these default positions:

- Curled up like a *Tyrannosaurus rex* (either one hand or both)
- Clenched or folded in front of them
- Behind their back
- In their pockets
- In constant motion

These presenters are using their hands as a buffer between themselves and the audience because they're uncomfortable, and the audience will sense their lack of confidence.

The default position for your hands should be at your sides, or, as I've suggested, women may prefer to hold them loosely clasped in front of the abdomen.

To the audience, this looks like the most calm, comfortable stance. You may initially be thinking, *They're looking at my hands. They're just looking at my hands and noticing they're not moving.* Actually, that's not true. They're looking at your eyes.

If you're doing as I suggest in the next section to make eye contact, the audience will be focused on your message. They will be absorbing what you are giving them. And that's what's important, because this presentation is not about you; it's about your audience.

Use your hands only for targeted movements—for example, to stress a point or when you need to point something out. Once you've made the point, put your hands back down. This has far more impact than you might imagine. An observer of one of my presentations said, "I knew when you brought your hand up you really meant business, because you seldom did that."

Combining your pace, volume, and inflection (described more fully in chapter 7) together with hand movements and other body language is very effective when you want to emphasize something. For example, say, "And *that* is important," and as you end the sentence, bring down your volume and inflections, and bring your hand(s) up.

Master Eye Contact

In his book *A Whole New Mind*, Daniel H. Pink, who writes about issues related to emotional intelligence and empathy, says facial expressions are the most universal and powerful means of communication. When researchers gave a very diverse group of populations photos of people showing different expressions, the people tested unanimously understood what the people in the photographs were thinking and feeling solely through their facial expressions and even without clues based on tone, language, or body language.

Yet when those same people were asked to interpret what an extended hand meant, some thought it was a friendly invitation to shake hands while others were offended. When those same people were asked to interpret a shake of the head, some thought it meant "I disagree" while others thought it meant the person was listening intently. None of them, however, misinterpreted an emotion conveyed by eyes. For example, an expression of surprise (revealed by wide-open eyes) was interpreted as surprise across all cultures.

The fact that the expressions in a person's eyes have the same meaning in all cultures has powerful ramifications for you as a presenter. You can't fake a smile, and you can't fake sincerity. There are several basic principles for communicating with your eyes.

Make eye contact with everyone

In a scientific experiment, a subject was sent into a room where people were attending a party. On one occasion, the subject was directed to stare at various people during the evening. On another occasion, the subject was told never to make eye contact with anyone. Which person did others perceive as more frightening? The one who never looked at anyone. If you do not make eye contact, you are seen either as potentially menacing or extremely fearful.

Your audience will feel safer when you look at them, and when you look at them, you are less likely to appear nervous.

When you're talking one-on-one it's appropriate to maintain eye contact about 70 percent of the time. More is weird, and less is weirder. But if you're talking one-on-audience, you want to make eye contact with some portion of the audience 100 percent of the time.

Your job is to direct your audience's gaze with your own. You have to be careful to do this in a way that adds to your connection with them, not one that distracts from it.

I described in detail in chapter 5 how to make eye contact with small audiences (thirty-two people or fewer) and with large groups: With smaller groups, I suggest you make eye contact with each person in the audience for about half a second in each one-minute period, and with large ones, I recommend you divide the audience into nine sections and look at each section for approximately three seconds in each one-minute period. Since the movement of your eyes is less obvious in larger groups, you can look at each group of people less frequently, but you must hold your gaze longer.

I developed this technique when I was preparing to speak in front of five thousand people for the first time and worked with a coach who had a lot of experience in training Broadway performers. She explained to me that a gesture that might be very small when you were performing in front of a group of one hundred had to be bigger when there were one thousand people in the audience and much bigger for ten thousand.

When presenters look at an audience, they tend to notice the person who is smiling the most or from whom they're getting the most response. Then they make the mistake of looking only at that person or persons for most of the presentation.

I call it a mistake because when you single out particular persons, you may alienate the others in the audience. And those others—the ones who are not smiling, the ones who don't appear to be reacting to you—are exactly the people you should be working even harder to engage. They're the people who may be on the fence about whether or not they like you, and you're alienating them even more by not looking at them.

Smile only when you mean it

A fake, pasted-on smile does not endear you to your audience. It's more likely to alienate them. Yet I see people do this all the time. In fact, some presentation gurus even go so far as to suggest you should smile as much as possible throughout your presentation. That's simply wrong.

A person's mouth may be curved upward in a smile and his or her lips may be parted in a grin, but if the person's eyes aren't smiling as well, people will recognize the smile is phony. As Daniel Pink explains, since facial expressions are the only universal form of communication, we are programmed to be very adept at reading them, and there's a physiological difference between a fake smile and real one.

To explain the difference, Pink cites the work of French neurologist Duchenne de Boulogne: "A genuine smile involves two muscles: (1) the zygomatic major muscle, which stretches from the cheekbone and lifts the corner of the mouth; and (2) the outer part of the orbicularis oculi muscle, which orbits the eye and is involved in 'pulling down the eyebrows and the skin below the eyebrows, pulling up the skin below the eye.'"

Fake smiles use only the zygomatic muscle, Pink goes on to say, because we have control over that muscle. However, the orbicularis oculi contracts "spontaneously," and only when we're actually experiencing enjoyment.

You can test this by looking in the mirror and covering up your nose and mouth. Now fake a smile and look at your eyes. If you were really smiling, your eyes would be smiling as well. When you're waiting in line at the supermarket, look at the magazines and check out the "smiles" of the celebrities to see which are simply posing and which have been photographed when they are genuinely smiling. The ones who are simply posing with a fake smile may even have a sinister look.

Bottom line: Don't fake it. A smile has to be spontaneous, when you actually find something enjoyable or funny.

Stay focused on your listeners

Rather than work from a script (and be tempted to read from it), every presenter should work from a blueprint, as I discussed in chapter 3. I suggest you have the blueprint with you on a lectern, table, or podium or in one of your hands during your presentation, just in case you need to take a quick look at it, but you should know it so well that you have to give it only an occasional glance.

If you glance down too often, or people are aware of your glance, they may suspect that you don't know what you're supposed to say, and your lack of confidence makes them uneasy.

To ensure your audience doesn't get the idea you are dependent on the script and unfamiliar with the material, I suggest that right before you take that glance, you give the audience a directional that takes their attention briefly elsewhere.

Some suggestions for directionals

Come up with a question about the material you'll be presenting next and say, "Think about this for a second." People will be preoccupied with thinking about their answers.

Tell the audience, "Look over at my screen." Everyone will focus on the screen.

Ask, "What questions do you have about [the topic you're covering]? People will be thinking about their questions.

Tell the audience, "Write that down." They will all take notes on something important you just said.

Say, "Take a look at your handout." People will turn to the appropriate slide in their handout.

Tell the audience, "Highlight that point." They will highlight a key example in their handout.

All of these directionals buy you time as the presenter to find your place in your blueprint while keeping your audience engaged and interacting with you, the material, and their peers.

To divert them for longer amounts of time, see the suggestions in chapters 10 and 13.

Stay focused on the audience

Occasionally, you may want your audience to look at something. If you say, "Hey, look at the screen everybody," some of them might in fact look at the screen, but most of them will keep looking at you. Why? Because you're looking at them. Where you look, they will look. If you want them to look at the screen, you need look at the screen.

At all other times, look at them. It shows you care and makes you look more credible.

Your Turn to Command with Your Body

Your facial expression and your body language alone can add a lot to your message. Use them effectively.

Review and exercises

Items flagged with arrows require action on your part. If you are uncertain how to proceed, reread the appropriate section in this chapter.

Take a strong stance

- ▶ Address your audience at eye level. Stay in the sweet spot.
- ▶ Practice standing in the proper stance and delivering up to five minutes of your presentation this way.
- ▶ Write, in your own words, what to do if your feet are hidden by a podium or table.
- ▶ Write, in your own words, how you will position yourself to include the entire audience.

Move purposefully

- ▶ Use the power of stillness.
- ▶ Practice at least one time consciously avoiding unnecessary movement.
- ▶ Note on your blueprint when you will use the power of stillness.
- ▶ Move from the sweet spot only when necessary.
- ▶ Note on your blueprint when it is appropriate for you to move.
- ▶ Use your hands only to give direction or emphasis.
- ▶ Note in your blueprint when you will use your hands.

Master eye contact

- ▶ Make eye contact with everyone.
- ▶ Write, in your own words, what you need to remember about making eye contact with your audience appropriate to its size and based on the guidelines in this chapter.

► Don't fake a smile.

► Write down directionals you can use in case you have to glance at your blueprint, and practice doing them with one of your takeaways three times in real time. If you are fearful or very nervous, practice it six times in real time. Stay focused on the audience.

► Note in your blueprint when you might need to direct the gaze of the audience away from yourself.

Chapter Seven

CONVINCE WITH YOUR VOICE

Persuade your audience with the words
you choose and the way you sound

Imagine going into a room making eye contact with a person, smiling, and giving a wink to make that person feel comfortable. Now pretend you're talking to that same person on the radio. Without being able to rely on facial expression or body language, using your voice alone, how could you welcome someone and put him or her at ease?

Or imagine you're a supervisor or teacher dealing with an employee or student who has committed a minor infraction. In person, you could just raise an eyebrow and look at him or her with a questioning glance—expressing mild chastisement without uttering a single word. But suppose you could communicate only by phone. Could you say, "That incident today really surprised me," and with your voice alone convey the gentle rebuke?

Yes, in both cases it is possible. Your voice is an amazingly effective tool, provided you know how to use it properly.

In pre-television days, Franklin Roosevelt was a four-term president. His first term began in 1933, six years after a brief illness left him paralyzed from the waist down. He taught himself to walk a short distance wearing braces and using a cane. For public appearances he would stand behind a podium, supported by an aide or one son at his side, but he could not walk and in private used a wheelchair.

Though he was unable to stride confidently onto a stage or stand at attention reviewing the troops he commanded, he was elected president of the United States four times, once during wartime, when a country especially craves strong leadership.

His radio addresses were what conveyed his strength and conviction. But while his speeches were always intelligent and inspiring, it wasn't only what he said but how he said it that mattered. Roosevelt's calm, reassuring voice was probably the most effective way he convinced the people they could put their faith in his strength as the commander-in-chief.

When people can hear but not see you, as is the case with radio, phone conversations and audio-only webinars, your tone is often more important than your words. Folk wisdom makes the same observation: "It's not what you say; it's how you say it."

To be effective as an oral communicator, there are three things you need to do:

- Choose your words wisely.
- Find your optimal pace, volume, and tone.
- Master inflection to create special effects.

Choose Your Words Wisely

When I say to choose your words wisely, I am not talking about the vocabulary you use to present your facts and ideas. I am referring to the categories of words and phrases that may reduce your effectiveness. For example:

- "Filler" words or phrases that make your audience lose focus
- Words or phrases implying deception that undermine your credibility
- Negative words that turn your audience off

Most presenters use some or all of the above. The good news is that once you become aware you are using these words and phrases, dealing with them is relatively simple.

Minimize fillers

Fillers—words and phrases people use to cover verbal gaps—are word crutches. Presenters often use them out of fear. They think, *Oh, my gosh, I just finished a statement, and now I've got to insert something during the silence or the audience will be bored and I won't be able to keep their attention.*

Some filler words have perfectly legitimate uses. For example, if I say, "I'm going to take this action so I can [get some result]," the word "so" has a specific meaning: "in order to." If I link two ideas—"We need to boost sales and we need to raise our image"—the word "and" means "in addition." But when I use "so" at the beginning of a sentence in a presentation—as in "So, let's talk about [whatever] now"—then I'm using it just as filler.

This is also true when a presenter says, "We need to boost sales. And we're going to do just that," or adds "all right" without any particular reason at the beginning of a sentence, as in "All right, let me go onto explain my next point." In these examples, "and" and "all right" are merely fillers.

"You know" is frequently used—or rather, *abused*—by speakers who are trying to assume a conversational tone and insert it over and over again for no reason. Two examples I recently noted when I was observing a CEO's presentation were double headers: "And, we make money, you know, this is no surprise," and later, "That's just, you know, it's how it is, you know."

The most common fillers are:

- So
- And
- All right
- Okay
- Like
- Now
- Well

- You know
- Right
- Um
- Uh

These unnecessary phrases also constitute filler:

- "I believe" (Of course you believe it; that's why you're saying it.)
- "There is" or "There are" (Instead of "There are many solutions to that problem," say, "Many solutions exist for that problem.")

Fillers may have the opposite effect than what you intended. The word "right" is typically used at the end of the sentence, to invite the audience to buy in to a concept. Used too often, it can seem manipulative and be a turnoff.

An especially negative effect of overusing fillers is that the audience instinctively, maybe even subconsciously, senses you are using them because you feel insecure. This makes you appear less credible, which makes your audience less inclined to pay attention to you. They may even stop listening altogether.

Recently, I did an observation on one of my clients. From my transcription, I discovered he had inserted 110 fillers into a 110-minute presentation, an average of once a minute. I told him a reasonable goal was not necessarily to eliminate every one of these fillers but to cut them down substantially, to one every three minutes.

One solution was simply to become aware of how many fillers he was using by recording and transcribing his presentation. The other was to make use of a very simple technique: pausing.

People I observe typically use one type of filler over and over again, either at the beginning, midpoint, or end of sentences.

Remove fillers at the beginning of sentences

If you sense you're about to begin a sentence with a filler, substitute a half-second pause.

Instead of	Say
"It's a very important point, and did you see the recent figures from yesterday?"	"It's a very important point. [Pause.] Did you see the recent figures from yesterday?"
"Is everybody here? All right, let's get started."	"Is everybody here? [Pause.] Let's get started."
"The last step is to send an email. Okay, are there any questions?"	"The last step is to send an email. [Pause.] Are there any questions?"
"This is good business. Now, the important thing here is revenue."	"This is good business. [Pause.] The important thing here is revenue."
"Our schedule is wide open. You know, we can be more aggressive."	"Our schedule is wide open. [Pause.] We can be more aggressive."

Remove fillers in the middle of sentences

Rather than use a filler in midsentence, pause, but even more briefly.

Instead of	Say
"We have like a million pounds."	"We have [pause] a million pounds."
"That's just, you know, how it is."	"That's just [pause] how it is."
"You can buy, uh, lots of things."	"You can buy [pause] lots of things."

Remove multiple fillers strung together

Again, pause briefly or very briefly.

Instead of	Say
"And, it's like, we need to sell some more products now."	[Pause.] "We need to sell some more products now."
"All right, so the next step is imports."	[Pause.] "The next step is imports."
"And, you know, this is no surprise,"	[Pause.] "This is no surprise."

Eliminate words that imply deception

There are four words and phrases to avoid completely, because they cast suspicion on anything you said previously:

- Frankly
- To tell you the truth
- Honestly
- Actually

If you introduce a topic by saying, "Frankly, this section is very helpful," what are you suggesting? That you will be frank from this point on? Or that you weren't frank about anything you've said up to this moment?

Similarly, if you say, "to tell you the truth," were you previously being *un*truthful? If you're about to speak honestly now, should I infer that previously you were talking *dis*honestly? When you say "actually," does that mean the ideas you expressed up to now were *fictional*?

Deal with these words as you deal with fillers. Just remove them.

Instead of	Say
"Frankly, this improvement is very helpful."	"This improvement is very helpful."
"To tell you the truth, this is a very effective product."	"This is a very effective product."

Use qualifiers

These two words can also affect your credibility:

- Always
- Never

A consultant was meeting with executives of a large company to present a long-term plan designed to increase employees' knowledge and comprehension more efficiently, to be well tailored to their needs, and to help them be successful.

When she made her fifth and final presentation, she thought she'd get her audience to acknowledge the importance of her plan and convince them to accept her vision if she used the words "always" or "never" to make her case really powerful. When it didn't happen, she was surprised.

"The first four times I presented this plan," she told me, "everybody loved it, but this last time, they completely resisted it. I can't figure out why."

"You're giving too many absolutes," I said. "You can't get your message across when you give an absolute, because that's what people focus on. And that weakens your case," I added, "because absolutes are rarely accurate."

For example, she had said, "The current training method we're using with new hires never works." There is rarely a situation when "never" applies. Worse, once you say "never" or "always," your audience automatically goes on mental alert, trying to find an instance that will prove you wrong. Instead of listening to the message you're trying to put across, they're concentrating on the search for one counterexample. They're distracted, and your message is lost.

Again, the solution is simple. Before using the word "never" or "always," insert the word "almost" or the word "may" as a qualifier.

Instead of	Say
"Your audience will never respond to that."	"Your audience will *almost* never respond to that." or "Your audience *may* never respond to that."

Find alternatives to negative and controlling words

Negative words seem to refute what you have just said:

- But
- However

Controlling words make an audience resistant:

- Not (or the contractions that include not, such as don't, can't, etc.)
- Should

When a sales executive says to a prospective client, "You're on the right track, but your customers still need more attention," the client may not hear the part about being on the right track but instead may hear, *I'm being told my customers are dissatisfied.*

When a CEO says to a staff, "You're doing a good job this year. However, you really need to hit your deadlines quicker," the staff may not hear the part about doing a good job but instead may hear only, *Uh-oh; I'm not hitting my deadlines.*

When you use "but" and "however" to link two ideas, the person you're talking to may even think you've made the first comment only to soften the truth that follows.

Your client may hear, *I'm not on the right track. He just told me that so I would feel better. What he* really *thinks is that my customers aren't satisfied.* Your staff member may hear, *I'm not doing a good job; he just said that to soften the blow. What he is* really *focused on is that we're not hitting our deadlines.*

Once you bring in the words "but" or "however," the point you make at the beginning of the sentence may be lost because the bad news following "but" or "however" is all your listener remembers.

The solution is another easy fix. Wherever you see the word "but" or "however," cross it out and insert a period. Then pause before you start a new sentence. The two ideas are no longer connected.

Instead of	Say
"You're on the right track, but your customers still need more attention."	"You're on the right track." [Pause.] "Your customers still need more attention."
"You're doing a good job, but you need to hit your deadlines quicker."	"You're doing a good job." [Pause.] "You need to hit your deadlines quicker."
"You're a good employee; however, you need to work on your communication skills."	"You're a good employee." [Pause.] "You need to work on your communication skills."

With the pause, the audience can separate the two points. The change is subtle. The difference in effect is huge.

As for the words of control, "not" and "should," one forbids action, which confuses the listener, and the other imposes it, which may cause the listener to resist.

The word "not" tells people what they should *not* do. They want to know what they *should* do. When you say something like "Do not use filler words," your listener may not know how to put that advice into action quickly. When you say, "Eliminate filler words," the person gets it right away.

Similarly, if you say, "Don't lecture to your audience," people only know what not to do. Better to say, "Make your interaction with your audience like a conversation." Your audience may still need instructions for the alternative action, but at least the goal is clear.

Whenever possible, give advice in a positive manner rather than a negative one.

Instead of	Say
"Do not forget your customer."	"Focus on your customer."
"Don't go off track."	"Follow your outline."

Finally, when possible, eliminate the words "you should," when you give directions. It is instinctive to react negatively to that phrase.

Instead of	Say
"You really should think about that."	"Think about that."
"When you're trying to get their attention, you should try pausing."	"When you're trying to get their attention, try pausing."

By eliminating negative words, you also speak more concisely.

There's a third benefit, too. You have guided your audience to take positive action by using a positive verb as a directional.

Find Your Optimal Pace, Volume, and Tone

A sales executive told me that what I taught her about pace, volume, tone, and inflection translated directly into closing more deals:

- She sounded more credible, which made her clients more comfortable.
- Her enthusiasm became more obvious, which motivated her audience.
- Her explanations became clearer, so her audiences were able to comprehend the most difficult-to-understand portions of her demo.
- Most important, she was able to motivate her listeners to take action— and buy her product.

You will undoubtedly have a similar experience. Even better, what you learn from the previous chapter about using your body language and from this chapter about using your voice can be applied not only to giving presentations but also to many other situations that may have big payoffs for you in all areas of life.

The effect you create with your voice depends on four components:

- Pace, which is speed.
- Volume, which is loudness.
- Tone, which is the quality of your voice.
- Inflection, which is emphasis.

To master volume, pace, and tone, first find your norm and then make adjustments to create the effect you want. (I will deal with inflection separately.)

Work from your norm

Everyone has his or her own "normal" volume, pace, and tone. Find your norm and work from that.

Volume: Your normal volume is one that feels comfortable and at which others can hear you easily in one-on-one interactions.

Pace: I have observed people talking as slowly as 93 words per minute and as quickly as 225 words per minute, but a good presentation pace ranges from 150 to 180 words per minute, the rate at which people think and brains process information. About 165 words per minute is ideal.

The actor Michael Caine says, "Subservient people speak quickly because if they don't speak fast, nobody will listen to them." In other words, if you go too fast, you seem desperate; you will lose listeners. On the other hand, if your default mode is very slow, you risk sounding dull, and your listeners will be bored.

If your default pace is in the normal range, varying it will be very effective. To convey enthusiasm and motivate people, you can speed up your pace by 10 to 20 words per minute. To present an exception or stress a point, you can slow down, which gets the audience's attention and helps them focus.

Tone: A good speaking voice is pitched low rather than high and is resonant rather than flat and monotonous. Resonance, sometimes described as amplification or enrichment, happens when sound is reflected by surfaces in an enclosed area. You can have a low, resonant voice by creating a reverberating chamber in your chest. This means taking in air and breathing from your diaphragm rather than from your chest. The diaphragm is the muscle that separates the chest from the abdomen.

Here's how to breathe from the diaphragm: Put your palm over your belly button and take a deep breath, pulling in air to fill that area beneath your hand. Exhale and let the air out. As you will see, when you breathe into the diaphragm rather than into your chest, you have a column of air power that can support your voice when you speak. If you speak while the air is coming out, your voice will be stronger and lower pitched.

Master Inflection to Create Special Effects

Inflection is largely a matter of where you put the emphasis on the word in a sentence or the syllables in a word. A change in emphasis can give a whole new meaning to a phrase or sentence. Look at this example.

- If you say, "I'm Jason Teteak," without putting stress on any particular word or syllable, you're just stating a fact.
- If you emphasize the first word—"*I'm* Jason Teteak"—you are suggesting that someone else may have been mistakenly identified as you.
- If you emphasize the entire last word—"I'm Jason *Teteak*"—you may be correcting someone who is mispronouncing your last name or distinguishing yourself from another Jason with a different last name.

- If you stress the first syllable of the last word—"I'm Jason *Te*teak—you sound very confident.

By varying your pace and volume and your inflection, you can:

- Generate enthusiasm and excitement
- Stress importance
- Compare and contrast two different ideas or things
- Re-engage the distracted
- Create a sense of urgency
- Appear knowledgeable and credible

Some presenters know instinctively how to make these adjustments, but I was interested to discover that these techniques can also be learned, so you can master the whole range of possibilities.

Below, you will find instructions on how to get the desired effect you want with your audience. Try using the exercises in the "Your Turn" section below to employ some of these techniques with your voice.

Desired Effect	Pace	Volume	Inflection
Build enthusiasm and excitement	Even or slightly faster	Up	Up
Stress importance	Slower; pause at end of sentence	Down	Up
Contrast two ideas or things	Varying	Varying	Up and then down
Re-engage the distracted	Varying; slow down/speed up Pause after important points	Up and down	Up and then down
Show urgency	Varying	Varying	Down
Appear credible and knowledgeable	Pause	Moderate, deep voice	Up and then down

Your Turn to Convince with Your Voice

Becoming aware of which words and phrases should be avoided and which qualities of your voice need work is a huge first step to making improvements.

Review and exercises

Items flagged with arrows require action on your part. If you are uncertain how to proceed, reread the appropriate section in this chapter.

Choose your words wisely

► Record your presentation and transcribe the first four pages.

► Circle every filler: so, and, all right, okay, like, now, well, you know, right, um, uh.

► Circle every use of language that implies deception: frankly, to tell you the truth, honestly, actually.

► Circle every absolute: always, never.

► Circle every negative and controlling word: but, however, not (and related words such as don't and can't), should.

You will most likely discover you need to address only one or possibly two of these areas.

► If you use a lot of fillers: Mark the text as suggested to omit fillers or note a (P) where you can substitute a pause.

► If you use deceptive, absolute, negative, or controlling words or phrases, mark the text as suggested or consider alternates.

► Rerecord the pages. Compare the two versions of the recording. Of course you won't be reading from your script word for word, but you want to be aware how to make your words more convincing.

Find your optimal pace, volume, and tone

► Listen to the recording you have made—or, better still, have someone come to your presentation—and address the following points.

► Transcribe one minute of your recording and calculate how many words you are speaking per minute.

► Determine whether you need to speed or slow your pace (calibrate to 150–180 words per minute).

► Determine whether you need to work on changing your volume.

► Determine whether you need to work on your tone and resonance.

Master inflection to create special effects

► Look at a page of the transcript you have prepared above. Go through the transcribed page, circle one key word every thirty to fifty words, and decide what effect you want to get when you are delivering that word.

► For each circled word, address the following points.

► Refer to the chart at the end of this chapter to help you decide what feeling you want to get across with that particular word.

► For practice, change volume, pace, and inflection in an exaggerated way to get that feeling across.

► When you're done, reread the entire page.

► Once you have practiced until you feel comfortable, read and rerecord the entire presentation and see if you have conveyed the effect you intended.

Chapter Eight

OVERCOME YOUR PRESENTATION FEARS

Stay calm and in control in front of every audience

A Gallup poll confirmed that the greatest fear of 40 percent of Americans is public speaking. It comes as no surprise that many of the people who consult me for help in making presentations express such concerns.

"No other advice you give me will matter until I can overcome my fear," said one client. "Once it sets in, I can't think about anything else."

If you've had only negative experiences related to public speaking, you may doubt I can turn things around for you in this area. But the Rule the Room method has done it for others, and I know it can do the same for you.

When I speak to anyone about giving presentations, and specifically about fears and nervousness, there is one thing I tell them that immediately offers them some comfort: It's okay to be nervous.

You just can't show it. Simply learning how to appear calm will help you to become calm.

The place to start is understanding where your fear comes from. What are its components? For example, if you say, "I'm afraid of sharks," it may not be the animal itself that's your problem but the whole scenario you conjure up when thinking of a shark attack: the fear of being taken by surprise, of seeing the menacing look in the attacker's eyes, of knowing how powerless you'd be to defend yourself, of being maimed or killed.

After speaking to many people about their presentation fears, I have discovered they all come from three underlying sources.

One is the fear of making a mistake in delivering the presentation: stumbling over words, forgetting what you meant to say, inadvertently skipping over a portion, or misspeaking in some other way.

A second is the fear of being humiliated by appearing inept, awkward, and uneasy to your audience. That not only would be personally embarrassing but also would undermine your credibility as a presenter.

A third is the fear of failing at your main purpose: connecting with your audience and delivering your message effectively.

You can eliminate all those fears and appear less nervous as an additional benefit by learning how to:

- Minimize the chance of a misstep.
- Channel your strengths and not your vulnerabilities.
- Focus on the audience's needs and not your own.

Minimize the Chance of a Misstep

The number one reason people are nervous is they're afraid of making a mistake. They're concerned they're going to forget something, omit an important point, get confused about the right order, or simply lose their place. The remedies are very straightforward: proper preparation and sufficient practice. Though this is advice you may have heard before, in this case, I will guide you step-by-step through the process.

Work from a blueprint, not from a script

When working with two new clients, I began, as usual, by observing them doing a presentation. As is often the case, both worked from scripts that included every word they planned to say. During their hour-long presentations one glanced down at his script or at the slides seventeen times and the other did it twenty-four times. Each of those glances lasted from two to seven seconds.

They glanced down most frequently when they were about to change the topic, usually looking away from the audience to peer down at the script or over to the screen to check that they were in the right place.

The lack of spontaneity that's inevitable when you read from a script meant their audiences were often bored and disengaged. Worse, their frequent anxious glances downward or sideways revealed a lack of mastery of their content. At one point, when one presenter actually lost his place, there was the shuffling and rustling of papers and the awkward loss of momentum that is every presenter's nightmare.

The benefit of having your presentation in blueprint outline form, as I suggest in chapter 2, is becoming much more comfortable about your material. You will be able to explain the particulars of your presentation in an orderly fashion without omitting any important details. For each takeaway, you will be able to refer to all important elements—the tasks, subtasks and sub-subtasks (if necessary), your theories, your research, and your examples—*all on a single page*. You'll be prompted to cover every point and be comfortable explaining it to your audience conversationally and without being tied to a script.

With a blueprint to refer to, you should be able to give your presentation without having to glance down more than once every three minutes and certainly no more than once per minute. Of course, you can take a quick look "for free" as long as the audience doesn't catch you at it. The way to distract them is by giving a directional or asking for questions. In time, you may become an expert presenter who can go for five minutes without looking at a page for reference. Acquiring that skill will help a great deal in making you look less nervous and more credible.

Follow the 90/10 rule

It is a comfort to have all the material available in your blueprint for reference, but to be a really dynamic speaker, you should be so familiar with your material that only 10 percent of your brain needs to be thinking about the presentation content itself and 90 percent of your brain can be thinking about your delivery to and interaction with your audience. If you are only at 60/40 or 80/20, you will be constantly distracted, looking at your content rather than at the audience, which will make you appear nervous and distract your listeners. More important, the more comfortable you are with your material, the less likely you are to *be* nervous. You make that happen with practice.

The great majority of people can get to 90/10 after they practice a presentation *three times* in real time. In other words, if you have an hour-long presentation, you would stand in an empty room and go through it from beginning to end three times for a total of three hours. Afterward, you are likely to find the cues from this outline will be all you need to remind you what you have to say.

I did a second observation of my new clients after I had helped them create their blueprints and told them to practice three times. Instead of as many as two dozen downward glances, I recorded only four to six. Each told me how much less nervous he felt about making the presentation. Most important, both *appeared* less nervous.

Though three practices are enough for many people, some need more. I suggest you practice until you feel comfortable, but I assure you this will happen sooner than you might expect.

Practice away your last-minute jitters

Even when practice has gotten you to the 90/10 level, you may have some presentation anxiety. You're most likely to experience it during the first thirty seconds of your presentation and for up to five minutes after you start. If you can't do a complete run-through in real time right before you are scheduled to present, you can reduce your anxiety if you at least practice the *beginning* of your presentation.

Go through the whole opener, from "Hi" and your name through "I'm going to show you . . ." and continue into your first topic. I usually suggest you continue until the five-minute mark, since normally nervousness dissipates by then. However, you may want to go a little longer or shorter, based on your past experiences of how long it takes you to relax. Do the pre-presentation practice of the opener at least three times.

However, if you experience not just nervousness but fear—the kind that makes your palms sweat, your voice shaky, and your brain blank out temporarily—six practices seems to be the number that does the trick. (That's only a half hour in all.)

The best place to practice is in the empty room where you will be delivering the presentation, before everyone gets there. If that's not possible, it's useful to find a private space where there's a mirror. Face the mirror when you practice to check you're not exhibiting any of the nervous habits that I'll describe later in the chapter. Even if you don't feel nervous, you may unwittingly use body language that makes you look as if you are.

If you're having trouble finding a practice space, use this tip a colleague shared. When he needs a private spot, he locates the nearest restroom and retreats into one of the stalls.

By warming up and relieving your concerns about forgetting, practice will do wonders to calm your nerves.

Find a way to relax yourself before you begin

Some people find that exchanging small talk before they come onstage makes them feel more relaxed and comfortable. Phone a pal or chat with someone backstage if you can. You might even say, "Tell me something that will make me laugh," which is so unexpected you may prompt a laugh from the other person and respond with one of your own.

Or look at some favorite pictures on your smart phone. The idea is to do whatever you can so you can start your presentation without looking pained or fearful but relaxed and perhaps even wearing a genuine smile.

Channel Your Strengths and Not Your Vulnerabilities

You are more likely to be nervous about embarrassing yourself if you are thinking about your weaknesses rather than your strengths.

Marcus Buckingham, a British American social theorist, suggests you make a habit of concentrating on your strong points rather than on the areas where you feel deficient. I have observed that everyone has several subsidiary strengths, a couple of major strengths, and one thing at which they are really amazing—something I call your *crux*. This is the strength you should focus on.

Ironically, most people can't readily identify their crux because it's something they're so naturally comfortable doing they aren't even aware it's their greatest asset. But it's important you find and use it.

Identify your crux

Start by looking over the titles of the fifteen other chapters in this book. They represent fifteen other skills that help guarantee you will give a great presentation.

☐☐ Prepare an Irresistible Menu
☐☐ Create Your Core Content
☐☐ Map Out Your Message
☐☐ Add Power to Your PowerPoint
☐☐ Start with a Killer Opener
☐☐ Command with Your Body
☐☐ Convince with Your Voice
☐☐ Appear Confident and Credible
☐☐ Keep the Audience Captivated
☐☐ Make Your Presentation Enjoyable
☐☐ Tailor Your Approach
☐☐ Stay on Schedule
☐☐ Answer Any Question
☐☐ Minimize Distractions
☐☐ Close to Applause

Identify two or three areas in which you are strongest and check the boxes next to them in the first column. In addition, if you can, solicit an opinion from someone who has observed you do a presentation or agrees to do an observation for just this purpose. Then go back over the list and put a check in the second column next to the one thing you enjoy doing the very most.

Buckingham says a true strength is not only something you're good at but also something you love to do. Where those two things intersect—the place where you have two checks—is your *presentation crux*.

Right before you go onstage before your next presentation, remind yourself of your presentation crux. You will pay less attention to what you don't do well (and how your audience will respond) and more to what you can do well and what you enjoy. The confidence you get will be very powerful and help reduce your nervousness.

Identify your presentation personality
Another way to build on your strength is to determine your presentation personality type. I will elaborate on this in chapter 11, but if you would like to determine your type immediately, go to PresentationPersonality.com. Using

that knowledge will help you not only in delivering your presentation most effectively but also in working with people in general. And it also will help reduce your nervousness.

Eliminate your nervous habits

By 1960, 88 percent of the nation had television sets. This led to the first-ever televised debate between presidential candidates Richard Nixon and John F. Kennedy.

At the time of the debate, Nixon wasn't looking his best. He had lost weight due to a knee injury, and the pain from the injury, combined with the heat in the studio from the television lights, caused him to sweat heavily. Since he tended to produce a heavy five o'clock shadow, he used a product to cover up the stubble. This made his sweating more obvious. Finally, the light suit he wore caused him to blend into the background, so his presence seemed diminished.

In contrast, Kennedy, wearing a dark suit, stood out against the stage set. He looked fit, rested, and calm. It is generally agreed that Kennedy's appearance, more than anything he said, turned the tide of the election in his favor. Subsequently, people began to analyze body language, facial expression, and other cues to see what a speaker was communicating in ways other than words.

Nixon was a bright man and an experienced speaker. It is entirely possible he was not at all nervous at the prospect of debating Kennedy. But as I mentioned earlier in the chapter, whether or not you *are* nervous isn't what matters. In fact, sometimes it's a plus to be a little nervous and on edge. It can keep you sharp. What matters is if you *look* nervous.

I like to use the example of a duck. When it's swimming, underneath the water it's paddling like the dickens, but the people on the banks or shore don't see all that effort. They just see the duck gliding smoothly and confidently across the water. You want to create the same illusion. You don't want your paddling and nervous efforts to be obvious. Be aware if you display any of the habits that betray your anxious state.

The most common signs of nervousness

These are some of the most common signs a speaker is nervous:

- Shifting one's weight
- Crossing and uncrossing one's arms and (when seated) legs

- Pacing back and forth
- Rubbing one's hands, arms, and so on
- Looking away from the audience (up, down, left, or right)
- Covering or touching one's face
- Putting one's hands in the *Tyrannosaurus rex* position, in one's pockets, or behind one's back
- Loosening one's collar
- Overusing the mouse in a demo
- Blinking excessively
- Overusing one's hands with constant hand movement
- Laughing inappropriately
- Smirking
- Widening one's eyes for no reason
- Raising one's eyebrows for no reason
- Letting one's mouth hang open

Most presenters aren't aware of their nervous habits. Often, my clients will read this list and tell me they get the message, but when they watch themselves on video, they can't believe their eyes: they're guilty of some of these very habits.

The good news is you can achieve a quick fix to *all* of them by following two principles that are astoundingly easy to master. I have introduced them previously but summarize them below so that you will remember to call on them.

Stand still as a default position

At the beginning of your presentation, immediately take your position in the sweet spot, feet slightly apart, shoulders aligned with your hips, and arms at your sides. As I have mentioned, women may prefer to stand with one foot in front of the other, weight on the back foot, and hands loosely clasped in front of the abdomen. Unless your opener obliges you to move, stand without moving for the first ten to thirty seconds. Move your head only to swivel it from side to side.

Remember: *The less you move, the less nervous you will appear.* You will appear the most calm and comfortable when you are standing still, looking directly at your audience.

Keep your hands still as a default position

"Hand crutches," movements without purpose (putting your hands in your pockets, behind your back, or curled up near your chest), send a bad message. Your audience subconsciously recognizes that you are feeling hesitant, scared, fearful, and just plain uncomfortable.

When I tell you to stand still with your hands at your sides, I'm not suggesting you hobble around the presentation stage like a toy soldier. Sometimes it's necessary to use your hands for practical reasons, as I have discussed in chapter 6: when you've asked for questions and want to indicate which audience member you are calling on or when you need to write on a visual aid or use a computer to drive a screen.

You may also use your hands to inject dynamism and excitement—for example, when you're talking about something particularly hard to follow or understand, when you're making a very important point, or when the presentation has gone on for a long time and you need to keep your audience engaged. If you keep your hands at your sides by default, when you do want to use them to get the audience's attention, you will have that power.

By moving your hands randomly and indiscriminately, you lose the ability to use them for effect. Eventually your audience members subconsciously think, *I thought the presenter was making some kind of point by using his hands, but he just seems to move them all the time. So I guess I can ignore the movement, since it seems meaningless.*

When you're onstage, remind yourself to keep your hands at your sides by keeping each index finger gently touching its corresponding thumb. This is an acceptable, discreet "crutch" that has helped many of my clients.

Focus on the Audience's Needs and Not on Your Own

People often get nervous because they are unsure they will be able to get the audience to respond to them positively and that this will reduce their ability to convey their message. The way to resolve this problem is to remember the presentation is not about you; it's about them.

Use small talk to make yourself (and others) comfortable

Focusing on other people keeps you from worrying about yourself, which automatically makes you less nervous. Many presenters find that one way to calm themselves before a presentation is interacting personally with some of the audience members during the period known as welcome time.

If you're not naturally good at making small talk, here are techniques that will make it easier. In case no one will be taking you around to make introductions, look around for someone who seems inviting, and make your way toward him or her. People are most comfortable if they are at the same level as you, so remain standing if the person is standing or take a seat beside a person who is seated. Then do the following.

- *Introduce yourself.* People feel more comfortable with someone if they know his or her name. You can keep the exchange very simple: "Hi, I'm Jason. What's your name? Nice to meet you, Joe."

- *Ask a prompting question.* People love to talk about themselves, and it makes them more comfortable. When they're talking, you too will feel more comfortable and less nervous. Elicit some information with a question such as "What's your role here?" "What brings you here?" or "How do you spend most of your time?"

- *Ask a furthering question.* This invites more sharing and helps both of you feel even more comfortable. "Tell me about that" or "How is that going for you?" will establish a connection and reveal something about the person. That's why this technique is useful any time you need an icebreaker.

- *Paraphrase the response.* This shows that you are listening, and it's one of the most effective things you can do to calm your nerves. Instead of focusing on your anxieties, your brain will be working to synthesize what the other person has said to you and finding a way to rephrase it. Again, this is a simple matter of saying something like, "It sounds as if [paraphrase the response]; is that right?" For example, when someone told me he spent most of his time outside of work hiking around the Colorado mountains, I responded, "Sounds like you really like the outdoors." This was all the encouragement he needed to tell me he also loved boating, and his main pleasure from being outdoors was being able to spend more time with his family.

- *Close with a pleasant remark.* After a brief exchange, excuse yourself with a polite comment or two as simple as this: "I appreciated getting a chance to get to know you a little, Joe, and I look forward to talking with you more today. I hope you enjoy the presentation."

Your responsibility in these exchanges is not to talk but to listen and paraphrase. Taking the pressure off yourself to make conversation can be a vast relief. Clients often tell me one of their top goals is learning to feel more comfortable in social settings, and I frequently discover that the source of their discomfort is feeling obliged to produce continuous talk.

Once you have learned to draw people out and make them feel good by listening and paraphrasing, you are likely to feel far more comfortable in social situations.

What's even more rewarding is that you will raise the likelihood the person you're engaged with will feel connected to you. When people talk about what's important to them, they feel good, and when they feel good, they feel comfortable. You may even enjoy shared laughter, which is the best way to connect. In any case, when your apparent interest makes the other person feel you care about him or her, both of you will feel more relaxed.

Learn about the needs of your audience

Sharon, a client, told me she liked doing presentations because she liked making people successful. So I gave her an assignment for the welcoming period that might be helpful to you as well.

Find out what your audience has come for during the welcome

I told her to speak with people during the welcome period and ask some version of this question: "What's the number one piece of advice you could get from this presentation that would make it worth your while?" Then I told her to write down the person's name and goal (and, in a small presentation, even make a note of where the person sat) and tell the individual at approximately what point in your presentation the need would be met. Then I told her to say, at the appropriate moment, something like, "I was talking with someone before this presentation who mentioned he wanted to increase his sales. Well, this will do that . . ."

After her next presentation, Sharon said this technique had made her less nervous. Focusing on meeting her audience's needs diverted her attention, so she spent less time focusing on her own anxieties.

Uncover audience needs during the presentation

Many presenters have had the experience of being able to conquer fear and anxiety as they were beginning a presentation and then having those feelings creep back up on them halfway through. Despite all their preparation, stumbling over a portion of their presentations may have rattled them or being tossed a challenging question by audience members may have made them uncomfortable.

A client described climbing a tree and feeling perfectly comfortable until he hit the twenty- to twenty-five-foot mark, when his fear of heights began to kick in. "I got to the top of the tree eventually," he said, "but if I could get to the top while feeling as if I was at the bottom, now *that* would be an achievement."

I gave him a solution that, once again, meant changing the focus from himself to another person and that person's needs and concerns. Once you start thinking *What do these people need?* or *What can I provide?*, your brain stops focusing on you, your anxieties, and your fears and turns its attention back to the audience.

I have found that the most effective way to keep yourself feeling secure while you're working your way through the presentation is to use the technique I call *agree and see if you're right.* It is a variation of the *circle of knowledge* that I introduced in chapter 3.

The difference is the type of question you ask. The *circle of knowledge* question refers only to the main topic of the presentation, asks only about achieving success, and is open-ended, with multiple right answers. But for *agree and see if you're right*, you ask a leading question about any concept you're addressing at that moment. It might be a takeaway, a task, a subtask, or an example. Also, and very important, the question has only a single correct answer. (For a fuller description of a leading question, see chapter 10.)

The process, however, is the same as with the *circle of knowledge*. You ask the question and give everyone thirty seconds to write down the answer. You give them another thirty seconds to agree on the answer with the person next to them and choose one of the two as the relayer to share their results with the rest of the room.

Ask any relayer for an answer, and then ask other relayers in the room if they agree. If not, ask for the answers they chose. After a brief discussion, say what you consider to be the answer, based on what you've presented. All people love knowing if they were right.

This technique ensures you are meeting the needs of everyone in the room. It's extremely powerful for you in order to overcome your nervousness not only at the beginning of a presentation but also at any point.

After all, when they have a chance to write on their own and then share their responses with a neighbor, you are essentially offstage. While you listen to and interact with them, your nerves go away. Also, their answers will prove you're meeting their needs—another way for you to overcome any nervousness.

Your Turn to Overcome Your Presentation Fears

Preparation is the best way to calm your performance anxieties.

Review and exercises

Items flagged with arrows require action on your part. If you are uncertain how to proceed, reread the appropriate section in this chapter.

Minimize the chance of a misstep

▶ Prepare your blueprint if you haven't already.

▶ Practice your presentation three times in real time. Be sure to practice transitioning between topics and use of your PowerPoint clicker.

▶ Immediately before a presentation, practice away your last-minute jitters. Remember, practice at least the first five minutes three times; double that if you are very nervous.

Channel your strengths and not your vulnerabilities

▶ Identify your crux.

▶ Identify your presentation personality.

▶ Eliminate your nervous habits and stay still as a default position.

▶ Make a recording of yourself doing a presentation. Watch it and identify any nervous habits.

▶ Practice your speech three times in real time, making sure to use the default stance and keep your hands still.

▶ Rerecord yourself and see if you have made changes.

Focus on the audience's needs and not your own

- ▶ Use small talk to make yourself (and others) comfortable.
- ▶ Decide what words you will use to introduce yourself to people during the welcome period.
- ▶ Write, in your own words, how to create a prompting question.
- ▶ Write, in your own words, how to create a furthering question.
- ▶ Decide what introductory words you will use in paraphrasing a question.
- ▶ Decide what words you will use in closing.
- ▶ Learn about the needs of your audience.
- ▶ Decide what words you will use to ask people for what reasons they have come to the presentation.
- ▶ Decide what questions you will ask in the *agree and see if you're right* process. Come up with two or three and add them to your blueprint.

Chapter Nine

APPEAR CONFIDENT AND CREDIBLE

Show audience members they can trust what you say

I watched a presentation by a history professor who is well known in his field and extremely knowledgeable. He had given out evaluations afterward, and I asked about the results.

"People reported I knew a lot about history," he said, sounding puzzled, "but they felt I wasn't very credible. How could that be?"

From having observed his presentation, I knew what the problem was. Though he knew his subject very well, his language, his voice, his facial expressions, and his body language didn't show confidence. This is why the audience found he lacked credibility.

To seem credible, what you actually know matters less than what your audience *thinks* you know.

In the previous chapter, I explained how some people might be nervous but manage not to show it. More unexpectedly, people who feel quite sure of themselves may not convey that to audiences.

I interviewed a woman for a project management position that required her to give a lot of presentations. I asked her how she felt about speaking to groups of people.

"Extremely confident," she said.

"Do you give that impression to your audiences?"

"Funny you should ask," she said. "I was sure I did. But I recently watched myself on video, and I was astonished at what I saw. I paced. I slouched. I was even holding my hands curled up in front of me! I didn't look confident at all!"

"But you were?" I persisted.

"Definitely. And I assumed that's what I conveyed. But when I saw myself on video, I realized that wasn't so."

Just as there is no automatic link between being and appearing nervous, there is not necessarily a link between being confident and appearing confident. You may be thoroughly informed about your subject and comfortable talking about it, but you have to convince the audience that you are.

There are three ways to do it:

- Use confident language.
- Speak with a confident voice.
- Show confidence with body language and facial expressions.

Use Confident Language

Avoid terms of uncertainty

Here are some of the top words and phrases that reveal uncertainty:

- I think
- I hope
- I guess
- I feel
- Perhaps
- Maybe
- Try

- Kind of
- Sort of
- If you'll humor me
- Let me

Remove these entirely from your vocabulary. Here's why.

You say this	Your listener thinks this
"I really think that . . ."	"Why would you be saying it if you didn't really think it?"
"I hope to cover . . ."	"I want someone who is actually *going* to cover this—and do it with authority."
"I guess that . . ."	"I want to hear from someone who isn't guessing."
"I feel like this is the right thing to do here . . ."	"I want to hear from someone who *knows* this is the right thing."
"Well, perhaps . . ."	"I want to hear from someone who is *sure* about what he or she is going to say."
"Maybe we'll talk about that later . . ."	"Are you unsure this is important or that you know this subject well enough to cover it? Either way, I'm finding you unreliable."
"I'm going to try to show you . . ."	"You will *try*? You mean there's a chance you'll fail?"
"We're going to kind of cover this . . ."	"You aren't sure you will be able to cover this."
"The answer is . . . sort of."	"You don't know the answer."
"If you'll humor me."	"You need permission to tell me things that may be inappropriate or incorrect? And if I don't humor you, will you continue to do so?"
"Let me make a good point."	"You need permission to make a good point? Are you uncertain this *is* a good point?"

Use words that show conviction

If you find uncertain words in your recording, replace them with one or more of the following words or phrases to suggest confidence:

- I will
- I'm going to
- Yes
- Absolutely
- Certainly

Instead of this . . .	Say this . . .
"Maybe I will talk about that later."	"I will talk about that at two o'clock."
"You know, I really hope to do this."	"I am going to show you."
In response to a question, "Well, it's sort of like that . . ."	"Yes, it *is* like that, and here's the connection . . ."
"I guess you could say that."	"Certainly."
"Let me give you an example."	"I will give you an example." Or, "Here's an example."

When someone asks, "Can you do this?," give a response even more positive than a simple yes. Say, "Absolutely. You're going to get this by the time you leave today."

Apologize rather than say you're sorry

It is inevitable you will misspeak in some way: You'll jumble your words, omit information, or give the wrong answer because you misunderstood a question. When you're about to correct yourself, curb the impulse to say, "I'm sorry." Instead, offer an apology. There's a subtle difference.

"Sorry" is an adjective. Intentionally or not, when you say you're sorry, you call up an image of your sorry self. Saying you're sorry suggests you're lacking in some way, shape, or form, not confident enough to be the presenter.

"Apologize" is a verb. When you apologize, you're owning up to the fact that your *action* might have been inappropriate, which puts you back in charge and indicates that, although you might have made an error, this is not typical.

Outside of presentations and in a one-on-one interchange, it may be appropriate to say you're sorry, but when you're on a stage in front of hundreds of people saying, "Oh, I'm sorry," you lose credibility. If instead you say, "I apologize; what I should have just told you is [the correct information]," you appear to be in control.

Nor should you ever say, "I didn't mean to say that." Good presenters say only what they intend to say.

Show you know your audience's world

Some presenters try to win the audience over by asking to be pardoned for their lack of credentials and expertise. I watched a presenter who was giving a sales demo to a group of executives begin by saying, "I'm not a CEO, but . . ." Don't make the mistake of thinking that this makes you seem humble. It simply makes you seem less credible.

If I'm a CEO and you're presenting to me, you don't necessarily have to be a high-level executive, but I do want to be sure you understand my world. To look confident, you have to show you identify with your audience. If you preface your presentation by saying "I'm not a [whatever]," you suggest you are not knowledgeable about what they know. Therefore, it's reasonable for them to wonder, *How can you teach me anything?* and be unreceptive to your presentation.

In contrast, I watched Tony, a developer of software used by pharmacists to write prescriptions for hospital patients, speak to 150 of some of the most influential pharmacists and physicians in the United States. At the end of his two-hour lecture, people in the audience were coming up to him and asking where he got his pharmacy degree. Now, *that's* an example of a successful presenter.

In fact, Tony isn't a pharmacist, nor does he have a degree in pharmacy, but he didn't start his speech—and undercut his credibility—by saying so. When they judged him solely by his presentation, his audience was convinced he was one of them.

Acknowledge the expertise of your audience

On one occasion, I was warned about someone in my audience who might cause some problems. From the description of his personality, I recognized he would be a type I call a heckler and a resenter. (I will explain more about those categories later, when I tell you how to manage your audience.) I knew he was capable of making my job difficult. In fact, I was specifically told, "You're never going to be able to present to this guy. He's going to derail your presentation every time."

I decided to go up to him during the break and find out a little more about him. During our conversation, I asked what he wanted from a presenter. "I want to know he knows his stuff, and I want him to know I know mine," he said. He wanted to be convinced of my expertise and to be acknowledged by me, which is what every audience member wants. Once he had both, he gave me respect and he felt respected, so he was more connected with what I had to say.

To satisfy the first part of that request—to show you know your stuff—you have to do your research, as I described in chapter 1, so you know that you're delivering information audience members find practical and relevant.

You can acknowledge their expertise and experience most effectively using the *circle of knowledge* at the beginning of your presentation, right after your introduction.

Giving responses will give them a chance to look good and to shine in front of their peers. This makes them look more credible, and giving them such an opportunity boosts your own credibility.

Use directionals to establish leadership

Confident leaders can move their audience to action.

Does "Would you mind telling me what you came up with?" express confidence? How about, "If you wouldn't mind, we're going to go focus on [whatever] now"? Time and time again I observe presenters making such weak and ineffective remarks.

Instead, try this: "Tell me what you came up with." Or say, "Start focusing on [whatever]." These are direct commands. Some presenters avoid using direct commands because they don't want to sound too controlling. However, you can tell someone to do something without seeming dictatorial or disrespectful. (See chapter 10 to learn more about directionals.)

In any case, to inspire confidence, you have to show you *can* lead people. To be effective as a presenter, you *must* lead them. This is why I suggest you use directionals in your presentation when necessary.

All directionals begin with an action verb. Read the following directionals aloud and notice the confident manner in which they inspire an audience to interact and take action.

- "Tell me what you came up with."
- "Take a look at the handout in front of you."
- "Read paragraph two."
- "Discuss that with the person next to you."

Be prepared for slipups

Just as I've suggested you apologize rather than say you're sorry if you misspeak, if you lose your place, do not blurt out something like "I forgot what I was going to say" or "I lost my train of thought."

Instead, just pause for three seconds. If you can recover, then just move right along. Otherwise:

- Ask your audience what questions they might have. This will work well if you stumble at a point when asking for questions seems appropriate.
- Give the audience a directional. Show them the PowerPoint presentation, for example, and say, "Take a look at that." Or ask audience members to take a look at the handout. While they look, the attention is off you, and you have bought a few seconds to recover your thought.
- Or move to another topic.

Whatever you do, do not announce you forgot what you were going to say.

Speak with a Confident Voice

When I coach presenters, I always ask them if they're feeling ready to present with confidence. If they say yes, I ask how they can tell.

"I know what I'm going to say," they respond.

"Good," I answer. "You've taken the *first* step."

They look perplexed. "What else is there?"

I remind them: How you say it is more important than what you say. To present with confidence, you must have a confident voice.

You show confidence in your voice through the elements we have already discussed: pace, which is speed; volume, which is loudness; tone, which is the quality of your voice; and inflection, which is a change in pitch or tone. Let me revisit some of the aspects of voice I discussed in chapter 6, but with a special emphasis on expressing confidence.

Speak at a comfortable volume

The most common mistake presenters make when they are trying to get people to listen is to talk louder. But you won't inspire confidence if you appear to be straining to be heard. If you want to make absolutely sure people can hear you, make sure a microphone is available. If you have a chance to come into the room ahead of time to find the sweet spot, also make sure the microphone is working.

Speak at a comfortable pace

Confident people don't rush. You don't have to talk at a rapid pace to get people to listen to you. In fact, one of the most effective ways to appear confident is to talk at a relaxed pace. The ideal pace is between 150 and 180 words per minute. A faster speed conveys enthusiasm, and too slow a speed may bore your audience. The most confident voice is right in the middle.

Use the power of the pause

We've already discussed how the pause can be used to eliminate fillers and help you speak well. It can also be used to make you appear more confident. Being able to look at an audience directly, to hold your gaze and not to show any discomfort during a few moments of silence, have a very powerful effect. You may want to use such a moment to indicate what you have just said is so important or complex that you are giving the audience time to absorb it.

It is absolutely okay for you to stand in front of your audience briefly without saying anything at all. Oddly, when presenters are asked how they feel about using pauses, they say they think pausing makes them look stupid. But when you survey audience members about their reactions to pausing, they say people who pause from time to time seem more intelligent.

What's more, from reading evaluations, I have discovered that audiences *like* presenters to pause occasionally. Those little breaks in time give the audience a moment to think.

A client was concerned that deliberately inserting pauses would seem artificial and be inappropriate for his audience, but once he tried it, he reported the extra silence wasn't awkward. "It felt natural," he said. You will come to the same conclusion.

Work on developing a low and resonant tone

The voice that conveys confidence is low and resonant. This may not be your customary speaking voice, but you should work on developing it, as I have described in chapter 7.

There is no better example of a low, resonant voice than that of actor James Earl Jones, who played Mufasa in *The Lion King* and Darth Vader in *Star Wars.* Actresses who speak in low, resonant voices include the young Kathleen Turner, Sigourney Weaver, and Jane Fonda.

One of the qualifications for being a newscaster is having a low and resonant voice because it inspires confidence. Look at newscasts of commentary by the late Walter Cronkite or by Diane Sawyer.

You can definitely change the tone of your voice. Katie Couric is a good example. When she was hosting the *Today* show, she had more of a breathy voice, but she made a change when she became a network newscaster.

If you're speaking before a crowd, you are likely to be using a microphone, which will emphasize whatever quality your voice has. If you have a resonant voice, the mic will make it seem lower and more resonant; if you have a high, breathy voice, that too will be amplified. You can see why it's very important to learn how to breathe from your diaphragm if you'll be doing a lot of presentations.

Eliminate upspeak

I described the many ways you can vary your inflection for positive use in chapter 7. The wrong use of inflection can also have a negative influence, especially when you are trying to project confidence.

I am referring specifically to what is called the Valley girl speech pattern—a reference to Frank Zappa's 1982 single, "Valley Girl." In the background of the song, you can hear Zappa's then-fourteen-year-old daughter speaking Valley speak. It includes slang and surfer terms, lots of fillers such as "like," and—most significantly—a distinctive pattern of inflection called upspeak.

Upspeak is a rise in inflection at the end of every sentence that transforms a statement into a question. Instead of saying, "I'm coming home tomorrow. I plan to stay for the weekend. I want to see some friends during my stay," the speaker says something that sounds like, "I'm coming home *tomorrow?* I plan to stay for the *weekend?* I want to see some friends during my *stay?*"

Unfortunately, this Valley speak pattern has made its way into mainstream speech and even into the voices of many presenters. Since it suggests hesitancy, deference, and uncertainly on the part of the speaker, you should eliminate it completely.

Show Confidence with Body Language and Facial Expressions

I consulted for a company whose key people were presenting an annual review. They had labored over their speeches for weeks and rehearsed them to the point where they could deliver them flawlessly. But when they actually presented, I saw all these behaviors: keeping their faces down and eyes glued to the script, walking backward, looking at only one side of the room, pacing, and so on. Some were hunched up as if they were suddenly stripped naked, and a few even appeared to be in pain. In short, they appeared so uncomfortable that I and others around me actually had a hard time watching them. They certainly didn't win our confidence and respect.

Yet when I asked how they thought they had done, most were satisfied. Some were pleased simply to have gotten through their presentations without getting physically ill, and others gave themselves good reviews simply because they remembered everything they'd intended to say.

"Not good enough," I said to them, repeating my mantra: *It's not about you; it's about your audience.* When I described the reactions they had provoked in the audience, they realized they had things to learn. Here's what I taught them.

Take a confident stance

To review, these are the key features of a confident stance:

- You're balanced. Stand with your feet shoulder-width apart and pointed slightly outward in a V shape.
- You're composed: Stand with both arms at your sides.

- You're erect. Stand tall and with your shoulders back. You don't have to be ramrod-straight, but you should not be slouching.

Though the above stance works for both men and women, I've mentioned that some women prefer an alternative that you may notice many television newswomen employ. It too shows confidence.

- Instead of standing with your feet side by side, put one foot in front of the other, front foot facing forward, back foot turned out slightly. Keep the weight on the back foot.
- Instead of standing with your arms at your sides, keep them loosely clasped in front of your abdomen to seem more approachable. Don't intertwine your fingers, or you may appear to be tensely gripping your hands.

Stay silent while you're in motion

One of the most effective ways to display confidence and emphasize your point is to say, "Think about that," and then stop talking. If crossing the stage for a demonstration will take only two or three seconds, remain silent when you cross the stage, take your new position, and turn. Then, resume speaking.

During the short time you are in motion, you may feel an urge to keep talking; resist it. When you stop talking, people may initially wonder what's going on, but once they see your purposeful actions, they'll feel comfortable, and you will appear more confident.

If you will be moving for more than three seconds, however, the silence will become awkward and you should speak.

Keep your mouth closed

Whenever you're not talking, your mouth should be closed. There is a reason why the expression "mouth breather" is used to describe someone who isn't quite with it. Someone standing silently with his or her mouth agape does not look confident.

Never walk backward

Many times, I observe presenters who are doing fine until they get a question that makes them feel uncomfortable or uncertain. If they don't know the answer, the number one thing they do is look up, as if they're searching for the answer from above. The number two thing they do is walk backward, as if they're retreating.

These subconscious moves tell the questioner, *You scare me*, and the audience perceives a lack of confidence. Even if you walk backward simply because you're uncomfortable working on a very large stage, the audience reads it as a failure of confidence.

If your problem is simply being stumped by the question, call on the techniques I describe in chapter 14. If the issue is the person asking the question—if he or she is the type of person I'd call a challenger—either step forward or remain in place, hands at your sides, and let your challenger talk, even if what he or she is saying makes you feel uncomfortable. In chapter 15, I'll tell you how to handle these and other distractions, but your first response must always be to stand your ground.

Maintain eye contact

I asked a very powerful, very effective attorney if I could observe him to see what I might learn and offered to give him any tips I thought might be helpful. He agreed and also said he'd welcome suggestions. (In my experience, the worst presenters are not open to tips. They believe they know it all. The best ones always want tips and have an attitude that is open to learning—what I described in the introduction as the "white-belt mentality." Being open to suggestions is part of what made them the best. And they just get better and better.)

The audience stayed engaged while he was talking, but when he paused, he did something odd that interrupted that connection. He looked out the window. The audience followed his gaze and did the same.

When I pointed this out to him, he said he hadn't noticed the audience wasn't looking at him. Of course not: Because he was looking out the window rather than at them.

I told him looking out the window not only distracted the audience but also indicted a lack of confidence. Presenters are most likely to look away—out the window, toward the floor, or at the ceiling—when they have been asked a question they can't answer. They can't recall it or don't know it, and they need time to figure out what they're going to say next.

The audience may not know what your problem is, but as soon as you look away, they subconsciously know something is not right. Whether you're having a one-to-one communication or looking at an audience from a podium, failing to make eye contact can signal a lack of confidence. Understanding this, the lawyer agreed he should break himself of the habit of looking out the window and follow the guidelines for making and keeping eye contact. To review, these are guidelines I suggested in chapter 5: With a group of thirty-two or fewer, you make eye contact with everyone in the audience for about half a second every minute. For larger groups, you should divide the audience into nine sections and look at each section of the audience for approximately three seconds per minute.

Your Turn to Appear Confident and Credible

It is not what you know but what you appear to know that makes you seem confident and makes your audience find you credible.

Review and exercises

Items flagged with arrows require action on your part. If you are uncertain how to proceed, reread the appropriate section in this chapter. If you have not made a recording of the first five minutes of your presentation, make one now.

Use confident language

▶ Listen to the recording as many times as necessary to check that you are expressing yourself confidently by answering the following questions:

- Do the words you use show conviction instead of uncertainty?
- Are you saying "I apologize" instead of saying "I'm sorry"?
- Are you showing familiarity with the world of your audience? If not, how can you show familiarity?
- Are you acknowledging the expertise of your audience? If not, how can you acknowledge expertise?
- Are you using directionals to establish leadership? If not, where in your blueprint can you insert directionals?

▶ Write, in your own words, what steps you will take if you slip up.

Speak with a confident voice

▶ Listen to the recording as many times as necessary to check that you are expressing yourself confidently by answering the following questions.

- Is your tone low and resonant and your pitch low?
- Is your volume comfortable for you and appropriate for your audience?
- Is your pace comfortable for you and appropriate for your audience?
- Are you using the power of the pause?

▶ Write in your own words what you can do to work on areas that need improvement.

▶ Do you raise your voice at the end of each sentence? If so, transcribe four pages of the recording. Every paragraph or so (about thirty to fifty words), raise your inflection—but not your volume—somewhere between the beginning and the middle of the statement, and then lower it at the end. Rerecord the practice session. The idea is to get a sense of what it is like to use this.

▶ Review the chapter suggestions for areas where you need improvement and rerecord the first five minutes of your presentation. Compare the two versions.

Show confidence with body language and facial expressions

▶ Again, look at the recording of yourself presenting and check for the following:

- Is your stance confident?
- Are you silent when you are in motion?
- Do you keep your mouth closed when you are not speaking?
- Do you ever move backward?
- Do you maintain eye contact?

▶ Write, in your own words, what negative or inappropriate body language and facial expressions you need to be more aware of in future presentations.

Part Three

AUDIENCE MANAGEMENT

It's ultimately not about you: it's about them—the people in your audience. Ruling the room means keeping them engaged and amused—laughing, if possible—and feeling that what you are presenting is specifically for them. It also means showing them you're an expert presenter in keeping to your timetable, responding well to every question, defusing any distractions, and ending on such a high note that they applaud you.

Chapter Ten

KEEP THE AUDIENCE CAPTIVATED

Engage your listeners so their minds never wander

You have to show your audience that in order to get the information they've come to hear, they have to listen to you. This advice seems deceptively obvious. I tell it to people who've come to me for presentation advice and they nod in agreement, as if to say, "Got it." But they haven't.

How do I know? Because the following example is somewhat typical: Sitting in the audience while observing a client during her presentation, I noticed although people were pretending to look at the presenter, most of the time they were using their open laptops to go shopping and check email. Afterward, I asked if she realized they weren't listening.

"But they were," she protested. "They were looking at me."

"People can seem to be looking at you but not be listening. I mastered that skill in high school," I said. "Let me ask you something: Do you enjoy being a presenter?"

"I love it," she said.

"Are you bored while you present?" I asked.

"Not at all. It's stimulating because I'm active all the time."

"Which do you prefer? Presenting or listening."

"Presenting," she said. "I hate sitting passively while someone drones on—" As the shock of recognition passed across her face, she cut herself off. "Do you think that's how my audience feels?"

Yes.

I suggested a challenge: Find a way to keep the listeners in the audience as stimulated and engaged as you are as a presenter.

In his book *Brain Rules*, John Medina cites research that suggests after about ten minutes of listening to a particular topic, people's minds wander. No presentation can be a success if you can't get and keep your audience's attention, but you may have searched in vain for a method. Here are three keys to the solution:

- Ask the right questions.
- Address every learning style.
- Give targeted directionals.

Ask the Right Questions

One of the best ways to keep your audience engaged is to ask the right types of questions.

To understand why, you first have to understand something about the human brain. It is made up of two parts that operate independently. Each controls a different mode of thinking. Adjectives that are used to describe the left brain include "logical," "sequential," and "rational." Adjectives that are used to describe the right brain include "intuitive," "holistic," and "synthesizing." The left side recalls the past; the right can envision the future. We know this because when the left or right side of a brain is damaged, the person afflicted loses the ability to perform the related functions.

Excellent communicators know how to ask questions that work both sides of the brain. This spurs the neurons to fire constantly, which keeps people attentive. When a speaker is boring, the only neurons in the room that are firing are the speaker's.

You are less likely to get a response if you ask a question that begins with "Can someone tell me . . ." because it isn't specific enough to stimulate either side of the brain.

Instead, ask one of these four types of questions:

- Recall questions
- Leading questions
- Relevance questions
- Expertise questions

The recall and expertise questions stimulate the left brain, which handles memory, and the leading and relevance questions will stimulate the right brain, which is responsible for synthesis.

I recommend you ask one to three of each type of question per hour.

Ask recall questions to help people remember what you taught

"Do you remember the number one reason why audiences are hooked?" When I ask this question in a presentation, or on the page, I engage you. Whether you respond in your mind or aloud, you answer the question, and presto! I have your attention again. Why? Because when I asked you to remember, the left side of your brain was forced to work. That's powerful.

At any point, you can ask recall questions based on what you've presented. For example:

- "Do you *remember* the top three things I told you about this?"
- "How *did* I say this is going to help?"
- "What *was* the specific solution to that?"
- "Can you *recall* step two?"

Notice the italicized words. Each recall question alludes to the past. Good recall questions do that. They encourage the audience to start using the left side of the brain more quickly to get a correct response. Of course, the real benefit is it keeps people listening and paying attention because they are being asked to think along with what you are presenting.

When someone gives an incorrect answer to a recall question, presenters often respond poorly, using words such as "No, I'm sorry, that's incorrect.

Anybody else?" This sends a signal to everyone in the room never to answer any questions, because if you do, you risk being made to look foolish in front of your peers.

For you as a presenter, it is a positive sign when people in the audience are willing to volunteer an answer. No one wants to appear foolish by saying the wrong thing, so you have obviously made your listener feel confident enough about what he or she has learned to respond to a question about it. What's more, that the volunteer is making the effort to recall the information indicates he or she saw value in it.

Even if the responder learned something only partially or inaccurately, his or her willingness to speak up indicates you have communicated something to that person and that person valued it.

Rather than create a negative mood by saying "That's wrong" if the answer isn't totally correct, acknowledge any information the person may have recalled correctly. For example, if I ask, "Do you remember the number one fear of your audience?" and a responder says, "Feeling safe in front of your peers," I would say, "Ah, that's the number one *need* of your audience." Look at the responder so that person feels cared about, and then ask the question again, so your listeners won't assume the wrong answer was correct: "What's the number one *fear* of the audience?"

When you ask the question again, return your gaze to the audience as a whole, and swivel your head to make eye contact with everyone to ensure the responder doesn't feel he or she is being put on the spot. You gain credibility and regain the audience's attention by throwing them the question once again, and audience members have the opportunity to look good in front of their peers.

Ask leading questions to help the audience understand

In Bloom's Taxonomy, a classification of learning objectives, synthesis is defined as "Compiling information in a different way by combining elements in a new pattern or proposing alternative solutions."

A question that inspires synthesis accesses the right side of the brain. A leading question that inspires synthesis and gets people to pay attention must meet the following criteria:

- There has to be a right answer.
- The audience has not yet been taught the answer.

- The audience can figure out the answer.
- The answer requires some thought.

For example, once I explain that the left side of the brain stores memories and the right synthesizes, I can ask, "Which side do you think you access to come up with presentation topics?" and the audience's right brain will go to work on an answer. The question meets all four of the criteria.

When I hear someone in the audience say, "Ooooooh," I know the person has synthesized what the presenter is saying and arrived at an "aha!" moment. Aha moments come when people have put together information that's coming from you with what's stored in their brains in a new way and then come up with an answer they can express in their own words. When there is true understanding—and only then—synthesis is possible.

When the audience members come up with the answer, they are learning. When they are learning, you keep their attention.

Asking a question that requires synthesis is one of the most powerful ways to keep an audience's attention, and good presenters are masters at doing that.

Consider these phrases:

- "What are some new ideas for . . . ?"
- "What does it mean to . . . ?"
- "What happens when . . . ?"
- "What is the effect of . . . ?"
- "What's the difference between . . . ?"
- "Who could do this . . . ?"
- "When will [something] occur?"
- "When should you try this?"

All of them implicitly contain the words "do you think"—for example, "What [do you think] are some new ideas for . . ." A question containing that phrase either implicitly or explicitly prompts them to come up with an original answer based on what they have learned. That's powerful. Requiring synthesis will keep their attention.

Anyone in your audience who answers a recall question incorrectly probably has not been listening or has simply forgotten what you said. But if someone in your audience answers a leading question incorrectly, it's likely your fault. You probably didn't lead him or her enough. Again, don't correct the person; simply ask another question with a better hint.

If you get no response at all, you probably asked a leading question that is unanswerable or patronizing. A leading question is unanswerable if any of the following apply:

- *It's too complex or confusing.* Example: "What do you think the engineers at NASA were thinking thirty seconds before launch in 1997?" How can you possibly know what the engineers were thinking?
- *There's no single right answer.* Example: "Is everyone in agreement about this?"
- *The audience hasn't enough information to come up with an answer.*

If in retrospect you realize your question is unanswerable, then ask an easier leading question (give a bigger hint) or rephrase the question.

A leading question is patronizing if it's rhetorical or obvious—for example, "Do you think it's important to wear a coat in cold weather?"

If you realize from the audience's lack of response your question is rhetorical or obvious, quickly answer it yourself. "Do you need to wear a coat in the winter? Of course!" Continue as if you intended it to be rhetorical.

As you read this, you may think, *I don't ask silly questions*, but I bet you do. I would say three-quarters of the presenters I observe ask at least one question intended to be a synthesis question but that instead confuses or patronizes the audience. This is dangerous because even if you do this only once, the audience members may stop listening. Therefore, I suggest you prepare your questions in advance.

Ask relevance questions so the audience can apply what you say

When an audience isn't hearing anything that seems useful, they become bored, stop paying attention, and think *Why bother?*

People will stay attentive if they are getting something valuable from the presentation. One of the most powerful ways to keep your audience listening is to ask questions that help them see what you're telling them is immediately relevant to their lives.

Let's say I want to convince someone to buy a special sort of knife. I would say, "Look at how this works." Then I would ask, "Can you picture using this in your home?"

Any time I give an example, I ask some version of the following:

- "How would this work for you?"
- "How would this apply to your situation?"
- "How can you adapt this for your needs?"

If I were presenting to you right now I'd ask, "How could you use relevance questions in *your* next big presentation?"

You can ask relevance questions throughout your presentation. When you ask a relevance question, anyone in the audience who might have drifted away usually comes back. Here's why: Everyone comes to a presentation wanting to know what's in it for them. Whenever you can give them an answer to that question, you've got their attention.

You can ask a relevance question about any topic. Let's say you're trying to sell your audience on garden design. When you show a garden slide, most of the people in your audience are watching and listening, but some of them may be drifting off. Try adding, "How could you apply this plan to *your* garden?" Now you've re-engaged the drifters.

A relevance question also helps make people pay attention because it stimulates the right side of the brain: It has to work to synthesize the connection between whatever you're presenting and how it would apply to them.

You can create a relevance question at any point in your presentation by relating your question to the current topic hook or the main presentation hook.

For example, let's say the topic hook you are presenting to your audience is about saving time. Ask a question that will underscore what's in it for them to listen to your presentation. For example, "How could that save you more time *at your organization?*"

Or, suppose your main presentation hook relates to making your audience more efficient. Then, when you are in the middle of your presentation, ask a relevance question to support what you just said, such as, "In what ways will this make you more efficient *in your job?*"

When you ask a relevance question about their desired hook and how the takeaway addresses the hook, your audience will be more attentive.

Ask expertise questions to tap the audience's own knowledge

An expertise question is a question only certain members of the audience will have the knowledge to answer. Asking such questions acknowledges the depth of their knowledge and gives you credibility points for being aware of it.

Expertise questions also serve to get the attention not only of the experts (who will be thinking about the answers) but also the remainder of the audience (who for a change will be hearing from people other than you).

Keep the following key points in mind when asking expertise questions.

Call for answers only from experts

I was watching a trainer who decided to ask an expertise question of a group that included both nurses and lay people: "How would you insert a peripheral IV?" A consultant without nursing experience volunteered an answer that a nurse in the room then challenged, making for an awkward exchange. The presenter should have been more specific: "Nurses in the room, how would you insert a peripheral IV?"

Give some context for the answer

When the nurse gave the correct technical answer, many in the room who weren't nurses couldn't follow what was going on. The presenter needed to give some context by explaining that a patient who needed to be medicated for a lung infection would need an IV tube threaded into his chest cavity to deliver it. By giving the context, presenters ensure everyone understands the answer while also building their own credibility by demonstrating their own understanding of the topic.

Ask that the experts answer for the benefit of non-experts

Presenting to an audience of executives, non-executives, physicians, non-physicians and IT staff, I decided to ask an expert question of the physicians because I thought the answer would be an attention-getter: "Physicians: what do you do during your rounds?" One responded condescendingly, "You're the presenter; you should know." Of course I knew—I was simply giving the physicians an opportunity to demonstrate their expertise. But this response undermined my credibility.

Next time, I rephrased the question: "Physicians in the room, could you tell the people who are not physicians what you do during your rounds?" One of the physicians gave an excellent response, which made him look good and made me look good for inviting him to speak. Best of all, this approach helped keep the audience's attention.

Address Every Learning Style

If your audience is learning, you have their attention. To present your content so you get the attention of everyone in the audience, you have to make sure you address each of the four learning styles: Step Learners, Talk Learners, Research Learners, and Create Learners (see Figure 10.1).

Figure 10.1. The four adult learning styles.

This learning style model applies to all adults. Everyone can learn in all four styles, but not equally well. Each of the four learning styles is the predominant learning style of approximately one-fourth of the population, and everyone has a secondary learning style as well.

My learning style theory is based on years of experiential research. When I presented this theory to a group of educators and business leaders, one individual told me this information would have been enormously helpful to him when his daughter was a young student. When I described what he instantly recognized as her learning style, he realized she'd had problems in school because that wasn't the style in which she was being taught.

What's critical for presenters to understand is that we instinctively present in the same style in which we learn, which means we are effective in teaching only the 25 percent of the audience that is in our own learning category.

Before you proceed, go to TrueLearningStyles.com and take the Learning Style Assessment to determine into which category you fall.

Defining the learning styles

Step learners learn most effectively by:

- Having a structured agenda that lets them keep track of key points and their order.
- Writing down all the steps to accomplish tasks described in the presentation.
- Hearing explanations of the usefulness of every item on the agenda and in the plan.
- Practicing what they have learned—first with guidance, and then on their own.

Create learners learn most effectively by:

- Being led to arrive at their own understanding of key concepts, steps, and definitions.
- Taking notes on the takeaways and synthesizing information by putting it into their own words.
- Answering questions that require some imagination.
- Coming up with solutions based on creative questioning.

Research learners learn most effectively by:

- Reading and researching on their own.
- Having debates and discussion in small groups about the information presented to them.
- Having follow-up discussions with the entire audience under the guidance of the presenter via steps 2 and 3 of the *circle of knowledge.*
- Viewing visual aids and writing about the presentation so they get the big picture.

Talk learners learn most effectively by:

- Talking through ideas, experiences, concepts, and key points with others periodically throughout the presentation.
- Answering questions that require synthesis.
- Receiving guidance from the presenter to see how to apply the information in their worlds through eye contact and directionals.
- Composing and asking questions of the presenter and other audience members.

On the next page is a summary of the key characteristics of the four learning styles (Figure 10.2).

Notice that some of the learning styles are directly oppositional to others:

- Step Learners want someone to model the steps and practice with them, while Create Learners want to figure out the steps on their own.
- Talk Learners use immediate verbal interaction to achieve understanding, while Research Learners prefer to think through the process on their own first.

Use the *agree and see if you're right* technique

You can and should target every learning style in every topic at some point. If you can present in a way that reaches all four styles simultaneously, you will be much more likely to keep your entire audience attentive. I have discovered one tool that will help you do just that. It is the variation of the *circle of knowledge* that I call *agree and see if you're right*. It gives each type of learner the information

The Four Adult Learning Styles

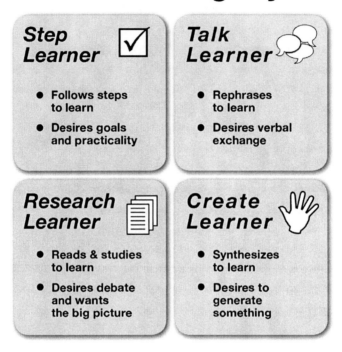

Figure 10.2. Learning styles: How do adults learn?

in the way they want it, it's incredibly powerful, and you can use it whenever your audience seems to be drifting.

As you may recall, you ask a leading question about any concept you're addressing at that moment: It might be a takeaway, a task, a subtask, and so on. Also, and very important, the question has only a single correct answer. It's a means to ensure learning (synthesis) has taken place.

After you ask the question, allow thirty seconds for audience members to write down the answer. Allow another thirty seconds for them to agree on the answer with the person next to them and to choose which of them will relay their results to the rest of the room.

When one of the relayers supplies an answer, you can ask the other relayers in the room if they agree. If not, ask what they came up with. After they have had a chance to share, you can tell them what you believe the answer to be based on the data and content of your presentation.

Here's how it benefits each learning style:

- The Step Learner gets the chance to see if he or she is right.
- The Talk Learner gets the chance to talk with someone about the answer.
- The Research Learner gets the chance to debate and agree on an answer.
- The Create Learner gets the opportunity to create his or her own answer.

This will give them an opportunity to see if what they came up with is right (which all adult learners love to do).

As you do this, you have recaptured their attention, and in the process your audience members will have learned either the actual answer that you give at the end or what the rest of their peers think about that answer.

When he first tried *agree and see if you're right*, a client of mine was astonished. "Even the very reticent and closed-off folks leapt right into the discussion," he exclaimed. I've seen groups of up to one thousand people erupt in conversation with this tool, which can work with any topic and at any time you feel the audience drifting away—as often as three times in an hour. Do it, and they're back.

Give Targeted Directionals

Yet another way to keep the attention of your audience is with a targeted directional. This is a short and sweet method that pays big dividends.

Whenever you want to get your audience's attention, request that they do one of the following, depending, of course, on what items—handouts, monitors, slides, and so on—you are working with.

You want to sound confident, but not overbearing, so they'll take action. You'll have no trouble getting them to comply if you do it properly.

When you want them to	Avoid saying this	Instead say
Look on a certain page	"You might want to turn to page five in your handout."	"Turn to page five in your handout."
Read a page	"I want you to read the second paragraph on page three."	"Read the second paragraph on page three."
Look at your slide or at you	"If you wouldn't mind, look up here . . ."	"Look up here."
Do something on their laptops	"And we're going to open up that window."	"Open up that window."
Look at their laptop screens	"If you take a look at your screen . . ."	"Look at your screen."
Think about something	"I'd like you to think about . . ."	"Think about that."
Discuss something	"I want you to discuss that with your neighbor."	"Discuss that with your neighbor."
Write something down	"Now, you can write down those ideas"	"Write down those ideas."
Highlight something	"All right, a couple of things I want you to highlight are . . ."	"Highlight two things."

You don't want to sound as if you're barking directions. When you give the directional, lower your volume slightly and raise your pitch slightly, and then bring down your pitch on the last word. You will make your point without sounding dictatorial, and the audience will be much more apt to comply. When they do, you'll have gotten their attention back so that you can start talking about your next concept or topic. This technique is subtle but effective.

Your Turn to Keep the Audience Captivated

Your audience will remain engaged when you get people to interact with you and when you reach out to everyone in the specific style in which he or she needs to learn.

Review and exercises

Items flagged with arrows require action on your part. If you are uncertain how to proceed, reread the appropriate section in this chapter.

Ask the right questions

► Create at least one recall question to help people remember what you have taught them.

► Create at least one leading question to help the audience understand what you are saying.

► Create at least one relevance question that gets the audience to apply what you are presenting.

► Create at least one expertise question to tap the knowledge of the audience.

Repeat this process for each hour of the presentation.

► Go over your script and find places to insert one of each type of question per hour.

Address every learning style

► Go to TrueLearningStyles.com and determine your learning style.

► Create at least one *agree and see if you're right* question.

Give targeted directionals

► Look at any previous transcription exercise. Be conscious of how you usually phrase directionals and how you *should* phrase them.

► Decide what words you will use to tell the audience to write something down.

► Decide what words you will use to tell the audience to look at something.

► Decide what words you will use to tell the audience to read something.

▶ Decide what words you will use to tell the audience to think about something.

▶ Practice giving the directionals using the tone and pitch as directed.

Chapter Eleven

MAKE YOUR PRESENTATION ENJOYABLE

Entertain and amuse your audience in a style that's true to you

People won't laugh unless they're feeling good. And they don't feel good until they feel safe. This simple concept has enormous ramifications for presenters. When people feel good and feel safe, they are inclined to laugh easily. Your listeners are much more likely to find your presentation enjoyable if you follow these three steps:

- Make the audience feel safe.
- Make the audience feel good.
- Make the audience laugh.

Make the Audience Feel Safe

Look at the Relationship Model (Figure 11.1).

Relationship Model

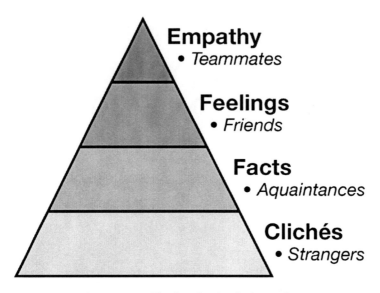

Figure 11.1. The four levels of relationship.

In *How to Talk to Anyone*, Leil Lowndes defines three levels of increasingly intimate connections between people.

- Clichés: communication with strangers
- Facts: communication with acquaintances
- Feelings: communication with friends

She adds a fourth level, as do I, but I define it a little differently. I think of the fourth level as the one that exists between an executive and his staff, a teacher and his students, a CEO and his colleagues, a presenter and his audience, where one person is interacting with many for a common goal:

- Empathy: communication with teammates

In an initial contact, a person or presenter is likely to make a cliché comment ("Nice day out there") or ask a cliché question ("Hey, how do you like this weather?"). At the cliché level, there's no real engagement. Real engagement begins to happen only at the feelings level. It deepens when you reach the empathy level.

Your audience doesn't start to feel safe until they get to the feelings level, and they have to get to the empathy level before they feel completely safe. My technique will help you get to that empathy level within three minutes of greeting your audience.

Step 1: Once you stand in the sweet spot and introduce yourself to the audience, you've bypassed the cliché stage and gone right to level 2. You're giving them facts.

Step 2: You give them your hook, which enhances their pleasure points (by offering happiness, success, and freedom) and relieves their pain points. With the hook, you're already at the feelings level. That's why the hook is so powerful.

Step 3: When you give your credentials without factual details, but only to explain what you'll do for your listeners, you're also connecting at the feelings level. For this reason, I've made a point of telling you to leave out the facts and say only what you'll do for your audience. The audience thinks, *Why should I be listening to you? What can you do for me, and how will you do it?* Once you make the audience believe you're there to help them, they'll feel safer.

Step 4: The *circle of knowledge* is the last step in getting your audience to feel safe. When you get your listeners to tell you what they want to know about your topic, and they learn that you're prepared to give it to them, they know you're all in this together. You're a team; you're at the empathy level.

Make the Audience Feel Good

When I was asked to speak to college students about giving a presentation, they were especially interested in knowing how to make their presentations enjoyable so they could get people to laugh. That's the goal of many presenters. I explained that people often make the mistake of trying to inject humor at the beginning of the presentation or when their presentation isn't working. That is a futile, desperate act, since people laugh only when they're feeling good, and before they feel good they have to feel safe.

As I presented, I gave them a behind-the-scenes insight that is always a hit when I speak about presenting. "You don't feel safe with me yet," I told them, "but you will. And none of you are feeling good yet, because it's too early," I added. "But in twenty minutes, many of you will be laughing."

I could see the doubtful expressions on their faces. But within that time, they were feeling good, and eventually laughter ensued.

The *circle of knowledge* always helps, too. Not only does it make people safe; it also makes them feel good. They have come up with the answers, and you've confirmed they're right. That makes them appear to be experts, and they shine in front of their peers. What's more, you've confirmed you're going to give them what they want.

Find your presentation style

Your audience will also feel good if they feel good about you. So it's important to endear yourself to the audience. You want everyone to be thinking, *I like this presenter. What a warm, smart, interesting person.*

You do this best by being yourself. Start by defining your particular presentation personality archetype. Once you do, and you act in accordance with that archetype, you can build rapport, have fun, and endear yourself to your audience. You'll not only deliver better, more credible presentations that get your audience to feel good, but also—since the archetype defines you not only as a presenter, but as a person—you'll be able to use the same skills in your everyday life.

Figure 11.2 shows you how to discover your presentation personality.

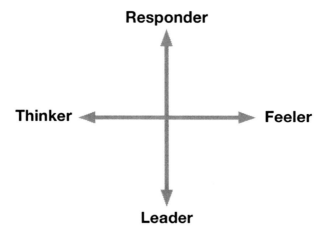

Figure 11.2. Discover your presentation personality.

At birth, our strongest tendencies are located in one quadrant. As we mature, we incorporate other styles, and eventually we have a fairly even blend of all four. But for the purpose of determining your archetype, think back to your childhood. Imagine your nine-year-old self. In which quadrant would you have fallen then?

Are you a Thinker or a Feeler, a Responder or a Leader?

Do you rely on analysis or intuition in dealing with people? Do thoughts or emotions guide your decisions? If the former, you're a Thinker; if the latter, you're a Feeler.

Do you prefer responding to needs or taking the lead, being responsive to others or initiating action? As a nine-year-old, at a birthday party, did you find it draining or stimulating to help the hostess set up the games or take around plates of cake to make sure everyone had some? Did you find it draining or simulating to initiate contact with new people? If the former, you're a Responder. If the latter, you're a Leader.

If you're still unsure of your type, you can find it by going to PresentationPersonality.com. There, you can take a test online to find out what your presentation personality type is.

Place an X on Figure 11.2 in the quadrant that defines you, and then refer to Figure 11.3 to see which category of archetype you naturally fall into: Fascinator, Inspirer, Energizer, or Performer.

Discover Your Presentation Personality

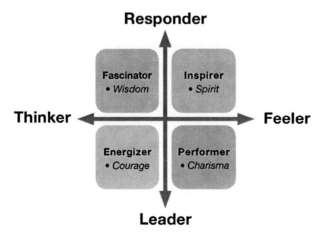

Figure 11.3. The four presentation personalities.

People generally yearn to be the opposite of their natural archetypes, though Inspirers can't naturally be Energizers, Fascinators can't naturally be Performers, and vice versa. When you take the test, don't answer the questions based on what you want to be, but what you are, so you won't try to be someone you're not in front of your audience. That won't endear you to them and may even alienate them.

Be Yourself

Once you've identified your presentation personality, you want to find the best way to be yourself in front of your audience and endear yourself to them. The sections that follow will help you identify and utilize your style's strongest traits.

Be a Fascinator

Fascinators endear themselves by sharing wisdom and information that convinces and reassures the audience they are reliable sources. Here are top traits of Fascinators:

- They endear with their wisdom.
- They excel at planning.
- They are encouraging.
- They are good audiences.
- They enjoy getting others to perform.
- They enjoy watching others have fun.
- They enjoy sharing trivia.

Examples of Fascinators include George H. W. Bush and Hillary Clinton.

I observed a Fascinator present prospective customers with his company's vision, culture, and competitive advantage. He presented interesting fact after compelling detail for ninety minutes, mesmerizing his audience.

One audience member noted that the Fascinator seemed to anticipate every question even before it was asked and was prepared with an immediate answer. Fascinators offer their knowledge and wisdom in a way that makes the audience feel they are in the most capable hands.

Be an Inspirer

Inspirers endear with their spirit. They use their intuitive and caring nature to meet needs. This makes an audience feel safe. Their storytelling ability and their talent for conjuring up the perfect story to make a point makes the audience feel good. Here are top traits of Inspirers:

- They endear with their spirit.
- They build rapport easily and on the fly.
- They are flexible and adaptable.
- They enjoy sharing their feelings with the audience.
- They are naturally caring.
- They read people easily.
- They enjoy sharing stories.

Examples of Inspirers include Barack Obama and Diana, Princess of Wales.

Inspirers demonstrate their empathy by telling stories to which the audience can relate.

I'm an Inspirer. When I'm working with clients in the field of education, I like to share this story about my first classroom experience. Having naïvely volunteered to teach a remedial math class, I soon realized the other math teachers had transferred their most challenging students into my new classroom. The principal came into the classroom the first day to help me out. He told the students, "This is your second and last chance. If you mess up with Mr. Teteak, he'll be sending you to me."

When he exited, I thought, "Great! I don't have to build credibility and rapport, because the principal did it for me. All I have to do is teach." Bang! Within thirty seconds, a desk flew across the room.

After telling this story, I conclude, "You have to build credibility and rapport yourself . . .or *desks may fly.*"

My audience thinks, *This guy understands my world*, and they start to feel good. They're starting to get in the mood to laugh with me.

Be an Energizer

Energizers endear with their courage. They have an ability to build up the audience's confidence and fire them up with energy to go out and get something done. This makes the audience members feel safe and good. Here are top traits of Energizers:

- They endear with their courage.
- They welcome competition and challenges.

- They hold passionate beliefs.
- They have innate leadership qualities.
- They have a powerful presence.
- They enjoy pumping up a crowd.
- They are fond of puns.

Examples of Energizers include George W. Bush and Sarah Palin.

Many excellent sports coaches are Energizers. They boost morale with halftime talks that make their teams feel good.

My friend Brian, a natural Energizer, became very anxious before presentations until he learned to use the Rule the Room method. Now he gives pep talks to audiences who have the same kind of presentation anxieties he did.

"I have trained dozens of people to look calm and confident even when they were nervous," he says. "Now they are able to get up in front of an audience and rock the house. I have done it for them—*and I can do it for you!*"

When he does this, he usually has audiences pumping their fists and shouting, "All right!" This is the kind of response only an Energizer can elicit.

Be a Performer

Performers endear with their charisma. They love the spotlight and use their body language, their voice, and their words to physically model key concepts and explanations. They can express ideas in a way that makes the audience feel safe, and they can engage an audience with their whole being to make it feel good. Here are top traits of Performers:

- They endear with their charisma.
- They can perform spontaneously.
- They love the spotlight.
- They get others to crave their performance.
- They can get others to laugh.
- They enjoy and feed off laughter.
- They are great at relating to an entire audience.

Examples of Performers include Bill Clinton and Angelina Jolie.

A Performer friend was the best man at his friend's wedding. He began his speech at the groomsmen's table, but within three minutes he had moved to the center of the tent, and during his speech he managed to make a 360-degree rotation so that eventually he had faced everyone in the room. He recited a poem, using his body and voice to maximize the impact, and he improvised as he went along. In fifteen minutes, he made everyone smile and feel good, and he got a rousing ovation.

Make the Audience Laugh

Everyone wants to know how to get a laugh out of an audience. Again, I want to make this point: People don't laugh because something is funny. They laugh because they're feeling good. And they don't feel good until they feel safe. To make your audience laugh, you need to learn how to have fun with them in your own personal presentation style.

Entertain in your presentation style

You don't necessarily have to be funny in the joke-telling sense, but if you have made your audience feel safe and good, and *if you are using a technique that is effective for your natural presentation style*, you will entertain your audience. When you do that, you will often elicit laughter as a result.

There are five techniques to help you entertain an audience in your specific presentation style. Your challenge is to come up with ways to incorporate those techniques into your own presentation.

Five ways Fascinators can entertain with their knowledge

Share trivia and interesting facts

I watched Ben, a Fascinator, mesmerize an audience with a story about a newly discovered planet made out of crystalline carbon —in effect, a massive diamond. After he spent two minutes describing this unbelievable phenomenon, one of the audience members couldn't contain herself. "Whoa!" she exclaimed, to general laughter.

A Wisconsin executive told his audience, "Did you know that the ice cream sundae was invented in this very state in 1881? Ice cream shop owner Ed Berners of Two Rivers charged five cents for the dessert he created, and he served it only on Sundays." When someone in the audience challenged this fact, the two of them had a good-natured debate that resulted in laughter.

Pose brainteasers and riddles

A technical professional put up a number of pictograms like Figure 11.4 and asked the audience to guess what song titles they were illustrating:

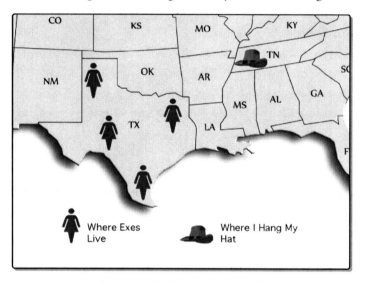

Figure 11.4. Guess the song title.

The song for this one, of course, was George Strait's "All My Exes Live in Texas."

A corporate trainer from Vermont decided to resume after a break with some cow riddles. She asked, "How many squirts are in a gallon of milk? How many miles away can a cow detect an odor? Waste from Ben and Jerry's ice cream is fed to Vermont hogs; what's their least favorite flavor?" (Answers: 350, five, and Oreo.) A number of these questions elicited laughter from her audience.

Share funny things other people do

A presenter speaking about anesthesia to project managers described different "recipes" that would ensure patient safety. To have some fun, she decided to share some "recipes" kids had come up with when asked how to prepare their favorite foods. Figure 11.5 is a sample.

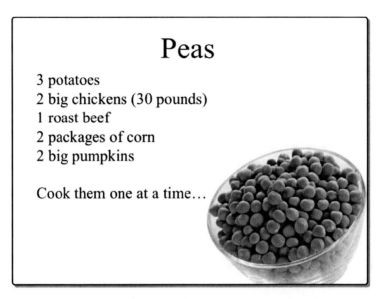

Figure 11.5. This "recipe" requires some imagination.

"No peas are involved, but follow this . . .and presto! You have peas," she said, to general laughter.

Plan surprises

A professor who was a Fascinator placed envelopes containing information related to her topic randomly under seats in the audience. Every ten minutes, she'd ask a section of the room to feel under their chairs for an envelope. When someone found one, she asked that person to open it and read aloud the information inside. She kept the audience engaged, and eventually any "winner" who found an envelope would get applause and laughter.

Tell analytical stories

I watched a sales professional speak to prospective customers about software implementations and fascinate them with details about customers, her knowledge, and her answers to the questions she elicited. She elicited laughter because she'd made the audience feel good about their prospects for success. Her audience felt that she understood them and the difficulties they had pleasing their customers.

She told a story about a physician who started out unwilling to adopt the software his institution had introduced but eventually became the software's primary advocate. Her audience of executives (some of whom were physicians themselves) laughed at this story because they could relate to it and because it had the kind of happy ending they hoped for with their clients.

Five ways Inspirers can entertain with their stories

Find a humorous story that is related to the topic

Here's a story a financial professional told to his staff that could be told by any presenter who wanted to make the point that using your imagination can solve a business problem. A shopkeeper was dismayed when a brand-new business much like his own opened up next door and erected a huge sign that read BEST DEALS.

He was horrified when another competitor opened up on his right and announced its arrival with an even larger sign reading LOWEST PRICES.

The shopkeeper panicked, until he got an idea. He put the biggest sign of all above his shop. It read MAIN ENTRANCE.

Tell personal anecdotes

To a group of educators, I was discussing the difference between how adults and children learn. I described how we took my toddler, Trey, trick-or-treating. He'd been given a bag of a candy at one house and was clutching it when we went on to the next. There a lady offered him a pumpkin full of more candy treats. He looked into her pumpkin, dropped in the bag of candy he had been clutching and walked away!

People in the audience laughed, but only because I waited to tell the anecdote after I'd delivered the third takeaway and they were feeling good. They appreciated it as an example of how kids think in different ways than adults, and it allowed us to transition to a discussion about the left and right side of the brain. But my initial intent was to get laughter, and it worked.

Use pictures and videos to illustrate your point

Before a presentation that related to change management, a project manager showed a video of cats interacting humorously with their owners or other animals. The video was a perfect tie-in to her topic—that different beings have different needs and styles, even when the beings are cats—and provoked laughter.

Insert surprising information

As I mentioned in chapter 6, there are two muscles involved in smiling, one that lifts the corner of your mouth (which you can use when you're faking) and another that affects your eye and contracts only when you're actually experiencing enjoyment.

In my presentation, I explain to the audience it is impossible to fake a sincere smile and suggest they check out the smiling celebrities on the magazine covers next time they are in the supermarket. "Put your hand over their noses and mouth and look at their eyes. If they're not smiling sincerely, their eyes actually look evil." Almost without fail, some people will laugh.

Initiate one-on-one conversations

Encourage an audience member who is sharing an interesting detail by paraphrasing what he or she said: "It sounds like . . ." The individual will feel good, since people like to talk about themselves. The audience feels safe and good because the wall between the presenter and audience is broken down when there's interaction, and an empathic atmosphere is created. This will often lead to laughter—especially if the comment itself is surprising or amusing.

Five ways Energizers can pump up an audience

Incorporate groaners and puns

I watched an attorney who was an Energizer make a presentation about selfishness versus selflessness. At one point, he said, "I just don't get it." He paused. "Hedgehogs." He paused again, and the audience wondered what was going on, because this presenter seemed like a very serious man. "Why can't they just share the hedge?" In a moment, the audience got it and started to laugh. Sure, there was some rolling of eyes, but there was a smile on just about every face.

Challenge the audience

A physician who gives sales demos for a health care software company walked into a staff meeting of five thousand people, introduced himself, and immediately put up the PowerPoint slide shown in Figure 11.6.

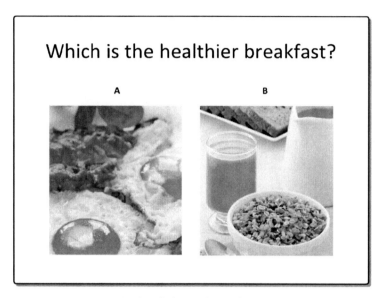

Figure 11.6. This slide got the audience's attention.

When he asked for a show of hands to indicate which breakfast was healthier, most voted for picture B. During his thirty-minute presentation on insulin, he declared that he had just lost thirty pounds on a diet that included breakfast A daily, because for his situation it was better to have fats and proteins than carbohydrates. The audience was hanging on his every word. I counted three times when the audience laughed, not because he was funny but because he'd endeared himself to them and energized them, which made them feel good.

Hold competitions

When Lauren found the mood of a group of about fifty corporate trainees she was working with often began to drag in the afternoon, she introduced a game. She told them the PowerPoint presentation she would show would include trivia questions, and she promised whoever got the most right would get a prize. Because she's an Energizer, she knew how to work up a competitive spirit, and she recognized it wasn't really the prize, which was just a token, but the competition that got everyone going.

She showed them the first PowerPoint slide with a trivia question and waited for someone to respond with the right answer, then noted his name. By the time she had posed ten questions, the same individual had answered three of them correctly. When she declared him the highest scorer and the winner, he pumped his hands and shouted, "Yes," and the entire roomful of trainees clapped for him.

Create team challenges

Halfway through a presentation about social media marketing, Joe, an Energizer, divided his audience into two-person teams and gave them a challenge: "You have ten minutes to come up with an elevator speech to get potential clients to buy. Ready, set, go!" Within ten minutes, all the people in the room were as pumped as if they'd finished a relay race. When Joe declared the winner, the room was filled with smiles, because the competition had charged them up and entertained them.

Give pep talks

If you look on the Internet, you can find a lot of inspirational ideas. For example, search for "You Can Do It! Ten Inspiring and Famous Pep Talks." I encourage you to write a pep talk of your own based on the takeaways you offer.

Start by deciding on the number one action you want your audience to take based on your presentation. Write a pep talk that will energize them to go out and take this action, and give this pep talk about halfway through the presentation, after you've had a chance to build some enthusiasm.

Five ways Performers can entertain with their talents

Do impressions

A performer who can do a credible impression of a famous person reacting to the topic at hand has a surefire way to entertain the audience. I watched a department chair impersonate Rodney Dangerfield on the spot as he talked about respect. The audience laughed appreciatively.

Recite a dramatic monologue

I once saw a project manager perform a speech from *Hamlet* in his presentation. At first, his associates wondered what he was doing, but he had chosen a speech that fit the topic perfectly, and the audience became totally engaged. He received a standing ovation at the end.

Do a stunt

I heard an educator promise the audience, "If you listen carefully to this next topic and I'm sure you've understood what I've said, I'll do a cartwheel." Because he had made them feel safe and good, he generated enthusiasm. Someone yelled out, "You're on!" The audience members listened, they got it, he did the cartwheel, and they applauded. He accomplished two goals. He motivated the audience to pay close attention to his topic in hopes of a performance, and he got the audience to ask him to perform.

Create a character

Some performers can use their body and voice to create a character onstage. When you're trying to put across a concept that is hard to grasp, this can be very effective.

I watched an administrator create the character of an imaginary customer of the type his audience would have to deal with. Then he did a skit, taking two roles—as himself (portraying a typical audience member) and as the customer. Not only did the audience laugh, but also they were learning concepts that really interested them.

Offer an actual performance

I saw a sales professional introduce a break by saying, "I'll tell you three things about myself. Two are true, and one is a lie. I can sing a country music classic like a Nashville native, I can do a soft-shoe dance, and I can play the accordion. You have one guess as to which I can actually do, and if you guess one of the truths correctly, I'll give you a demonstration." The audience loved having to guess. A master performer can get the audience to beg for the performance— and after the break, that's exactly what happened here.

I've worked with Performers who got the attention of the audience by juggling or playing a guitar. Though this entertainment may be unrelated to the topic itself, it's a great way to regain the audience's attention when they've returned from a break.

Be true to your style

You may occasionally borrow a technique that's best suited to another type, but for the most part, stick with your natural style. I cannot emphasize this enough.

When you do what you're naturally good at, your audience is much more apt to feel comfortable, feel good, and laugh in response.

Your Turn to Make Your Presentation Enjoyable

Make the audience feel safe and good so they will be amused (and even laugh) when you entertain them in your own distinct personality style.

Review and exercises

Items flagged with arrows require action on your part. If you are uncertain how to proceed, reread the appropriate section in this chapter.

Make the audience feel safe

- ▶ Write in your own words the techniques for introducing yourself and presenting your credentials.
- ▶ Write in your own words the first few steps to connect with your audience.
- ▶ Create a question for the *circle of knowledge*.

Make the audience feel good

- ▶ Find your presentation style.
    - • Identify whether you are a Thinker or a Feeler.
    - • Identify whether you are a Responder or a Leader.
- ▶ Go to PresentationPersonality.com to determine your presentation personality type and then consider which traits in your presentation personality type define you best.

Make the Audience Laugh

- ▶ Add three fun elements during a one- to two-hour presentation.
    - • If you are a Fascinator, find three specific ways to entertain with your knowledge.
    - • If you are an Inspirer, find three specific ways to entertain with your stories.
    - • If you are an Energizer, find three specific ways you can pump up your audience.
    - • If you are a Performer, find three specific ways to entertain with your talents.

Chapter Twelve

TAILOR YOUR APPROACH

Make all listeners feel your message is meant just for them

You may routinely give presentations on different topics to a particular kind of audience (a group of physicians, for example, or executives, or even a convocation of college students). You may also give presentations on the same topic to audiences of all different types. In either case, there will be times when you want to make the presentation even more effective by spending some advance time tailoring it for a specific audience.

It's even more challenging when you arrive at a presentation only to discover the composition of your audience is not what you expected. Or, even if you've done your research and prepared very carefully for your audience, you realize that their expectations are different from what you had anticipated. In these cases, you'll also have to tailor your presentation, but you'll have to do it in real time.

Here are ways to meet both sets of challenges:

- Edit in advance for specific audiences.
- Spot the signs that your audience needs a spark.
- Be prepared to customize on the fly.

Tailoring your approach will give your presentation much extra added value.

Edit in Advance for Specific Audiences

I am surprised when I look over presentations and discover that presenters have not done enough work to ensure their stories and examples are customized according to the particular requirements of the audience. Your audience needs to feel as if you have written this presentation specifically for them—even if that's not the case.

Customize takeaway hooks for your listeners

If you are giving the same presentation to a number of different audiences, one of the best ways to make your listeners feel you wrote the presentation just for them is to modify every one of your takeaway hooks to suit them in particular.

For example, when I gave a presentation to a group of newly hired assistant professors on how to give a compelling lecture, among the takeaways I planned to include was one about confidence.

Typically, I'd introduce the hook by saying, "I'm going to show you how to come across as completely confident, safe, and trustworthy." For the professors, I rephrased the topic so it would appear to be tailored to them: "I'm going to show you how to feel and show more confidence and credibility so you and your students can focus more on learning."

When I delivered this hook, the professors were especially attentive and engaged.

Do additional research for a specific audience

I have said you need to do research for a presentation, and if your topic is generic, it pays to do additional research when you're going to appear before a particular type of audience. I knew how to tailor my presentation to what the professors wanted because a few weeks prior to the presentation, I had called on some of them to discuss what would be important to their peers. I asked the sort of questions I suggested in chapter 1—questions that elicited some of their pain points and pleasure points:

- *What most worries assistant professors about giving a lecture?* The number one answer? They were concerned about appearing credible to the students.
- *What are your biggest challenges as lecturers?* Covering the entire topic was one. Dealing with different levels of competence in a single classroom was another.
- *What were some of the problems the challenge causes?* Being ignored by students who were sitting with their computers open to Facebook. Feeling their confidence erode. Worrying about their competence as teachers.
- *What would be the ideal outcome after attending a presentation on giving a compelling lecture?* They described it as having confidence that they could appear before seventy-five students with open laptops, call them to attention, and manage to keep their attention for an hour.
- *What would getting such an outcome do for you?* Feeling confident would make them enjoy interacting with their students and have a snowball effect, they told me. They'd become better teachers and could focus on helping the students learn.

These answers helped me tailor my hooks so I could make the audience crave what I was going to say.

Customize your title slide

If you have tweaked the name of the title, make sure it appears correctly on the slide that will be onscreen when people enter. To convey to your audience that this presentation is not generic but intended specifically for them and their needs, add a subtitle referring to the audience (I described it as the audience identification in chapter 3). The slide shown in Figure 12.1 was for an audience of assistant professors. If you were presenting to school administrators, it would read, "Ideas for School Administrators"; to personal trainers, "Ideas for Personal Trainers"; and so on.

Consider the sensibilities of the group you're addressing

For perhaps the first time in history, we have four generations in the workplace at the same time: Traditionalists, born before World War II; Baby Boomers, born between the early 1940s and the early 1960s; Generation X, born in the

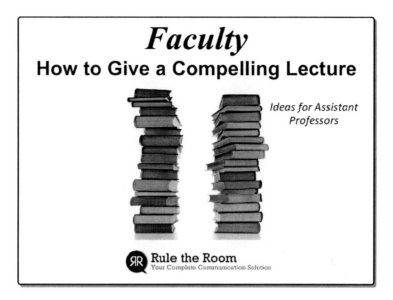

Figure 12.1. Title slide tailored to assistant professors.

late 1960s and in the 1970s, and the Millennials, born during the 1980s and 1990s. Members of any of these groups may understand allusions, enjoy stories, and respond to jokes that are lost on or even disagreeable to the people in the other groups.

Test out your material beforehand

If you don't know in advance what the composition of your audience will be, assume it will be a mixture, and plan to use humor, language, and references that will be understood by all generations. Don't be insensitive to the fact that some material might confuse or offend certain audience members for one reason or another. To make sure your attempts at humor will be enjoyed or your cultural references will be understood, test out these items on various generations, and ask your listeners to flag anything that is potentially objectionable, inappropriate, or otherwise unsuitable that you should either modify or eliminate.

Tailor your style to your audience

If you're speaking to an audience of young people, you may choose to tailor to them by using more informal language. With older people you might want to be less casual. But be true to yourself. A mature person may appear inappropriate and even foolish if he or she tries too hard to be cool in front of a young audience, and a young person may lose some energy and spontaneity if he or she attempts to be all business.

Plan questions that are geared to a specific group

There are several ways you can tailor your question periods for your audience.

If you're addressing people who are working in a corporate culture that's more freewheeling than traditional, your audience is more likely to enjoy interactivity, so you should be prepared to ask extra questions.

If your audience will consist partially or entirely of Traditionalists and Baby Boomers, you can assume your listeners will have years of experience in the field. Your questions might be designed to draw on that expertise. For example, you might ask, "As a leader in your industry, what are some of the things you do to motivate your employees?" Or you might say, "Based on your observations, what is the most important thing new customers care about in this field?"

Alternatively, if you will have some or many Gen Xers and Millennials, you might ask, "What area would you tell a newcomer in the field is most important to strive for improvement?" Or, since this group tends to be more comfortable with technology and you want to convey the idea the presentation is tailored to them, ask questions that relate to your topic that tap into their technical expertise. For example, "What are some of the ways you've used social media?" or "How can we incorporate technology into this solution?"

Be prepared to match the mood of the audience

If possible, do some advance research about the sponsoring organization that can help you anticipate the general mood of your audience. Perhaps the sponsoring organization is facing financial reorganization, so the staff is being cut and the people remaining are uncertain about their positions. Or perhaps the company has brought you in to implement new procedures and the personnel aren't happy about the changes.

Begin with a neutral tone. Don't try to incorporate humor or enthusiasm right away. People won't respond to humor or enthusiasm until they're feeling good. They don't feel good until they feel safe. And they don't feel safe until they trust you. Wait until after you've covered your first takeaway or later before you introduce any humor. They'll start to feel good only after you've taught them something that catches their attention and/or their imagination.

Gradually—by the end of the opener, after you've shown them the list of takeaways, and especially after you've taught them how to achieve the first takeaway—your audience members should become responsive. Once they start to demonstrate some enthusiasm, you can respond to it, build on it, and perhaps introduce some humor.

Spot the Signs That Your Audience Needs a Spark

Years ago, I asked a client what he considered the biggest challenge in tailoring his approach. "I think the most important thing is to learn to read the clues that what I've prepared isn't working," he said. "I'm always worried I might be droning on while my audience is drifting away." I've since discovered that many presenters share this concern.

In such a situation, you can still deliver an amazing presentation by abandoning some topics and substituting others—in real time. The key is to recognize the signs you need to do this and that you react—the sooner, the better.

Recognize the signs of boredom

You'll feel a lot more secure if you can gauge when things aren't going well. This is easier than you might suspect. You already have the tools. After all, if you were talking one-on-one with someone, I'm sure you'd have no trouble sensing whether the other person is engaged, because you'd spot at least a few of the signs:

- Making eye contact
- Nodding or showing some other expression that signals comprehension
- Asking questions about what you're saying
- Responding to questions you might ask about what you're saying
- Taking notes if there's something to follow up on

Now, imagine that each of the individuals in your audience is the only person in the room. If the presentation is working, each of them should be giving you the very same signs. If this isn't happening, you have to react immediately, in real time.

Be Prepared to Customize on the Fly

If audience members are unresponsive or negative, they're likely not getting what they wanted for one of two reasons:

- Your presentation isn't meeting the audience's expectations: It's not giving them what they came for.
- Your presentation isn't meeting the audience's needs: It isn't giving them adequate and actionable solutions.

Even if you prepared using all the techniques I suggest in chapters 1–4, it is possible your audience will want to know even more than you had planned to cover.

You can find out what the audience hopes to learn while you are actually delivering the presentation, and you can make sure to deliver it.

To show an audience you're responsive to them, the first thing you have to demonstrate is that you're listening, you know what's important to them, and you know how they're feeling. They have to be sure you have heard them before they will feel that what you are saying is meant directly for them.

This means they don't want you to offer solutions until they have asked for them, so your job is to get them to tell you what they want to know. Then, when they're convinced you're tailoring your approach to their needs, they'll be responsive.

Once again, I'm going to remind you it's not *what* they want that's really important. It's *why* they want it. You need insight into their emotional needs—their pain points and their pleasure points. You need to find out what is bothering them so you can offer appropriate remedies or what they desire so you can offer the means to get it. You can get that information quickly and effectively with the *circle of knowledge*. I've already told you how it helps capture their attention and makes your presentation enjoyable; now I'll explain how it helps you tailor your approach.

I was speaking to a group of deans at a large university and then to a gathering of student ambassadors who had been hired to recruit other students to join the sponsoring organization. In both cases, I was talking about how to give a presentation. I knew the takeaways for both would be similar. But I wasn't sure which specific takeaways would matter the most to each group.

I knew the *circle of knowledge* would help me to customize my presentation on the fly and allow me to focus on the areas that were of primary interest to each one. Knowing this, I could change my emphasis, a simple matter of taking time away from some topics and adding time to or emphasizing others.

When I asked the college students the top three things that make an effective presenter, one said, "They know how to deal with questions they don't know the answer to," and a second said, "They know how to interrupt the questioning to deliver their message." Those responses, which revealed their fears and doubts, represented their pain points.

I asked the deans what *they* felt made a presenter effective. Their responses made it clear their main concern was managing to communicate everything they felt was necessary in a relatively brief period of time. Again, they had revealed their pain points to me.

Show empathy to make them know you're tailoring to them

I made eye contact with each student as I spoke to them. I said to the first, "It sounds as if you're saying you want to make sure you don't look inexperienced," and to the second, "and you want to answer questions to make them feel cared about, but you don't want to do that at the expense of your message." Paraphrasing your audience's responses to the *circle of knowledge*, stating their concerns in your words, demonstrates your empathy.

After the paraphrase, I immediately asked, "Is that right?" When you paraphrase, as I explained, you may not immediately get an affirmative response, so you should simply try again. The process may take some time, but putting in the effort before you get a yes will benefit you as well as the questioner: It's extra confirmation to the audience that you're listening to their needs and it ensures you elicit the pleasure and pain points that will help you properly tailor your presentation.

Once you get affirmation, assure the person who asked the question by saying, "You're going to learn to deal with all these issues today." This shows those individuals—and all the people in the audience who have the same questions—that your presentation is tailored to them.

Point out the examples where you have tailored

When I talked to the deans, who were concerned about getting across their message with limited time, I knew I had already included in my presentation three takeaways that would help them reach that goal.

- Having a good hook.
- Speaking convincingly.
- Handling questions so they would be focused.

So, when I presented each of these takeaways, I made a point of saying, "And that will be something you can do in less than five minutes."

Every time you present a takeaway that will solve a concern (and thus relieve a pain point or enhance a pleasure point) that someone has specifically mentioned, remind your audience you are doing so. Make it clear their needs are being met and the presentation is being tailored to them. That's the key. You will become better and better at doing this on the fly as you become a more experienced presenter.

For the college ambassadors, whose concerns were related to appearing confident and handling questions, after I explained how to achieve a takeaway, I'd say why it was helpful: "That will make you look more experienced," or, "That will ensure they won't know you don't have the answer," or, "That will decrease the number of irrelevant questions you get." Every time I did this, I noticed more eye contact, more nodding, more questions, more answers, and more note taking. I could sense the audience's respect growing each time it appeared I had created this presentation just for them, which in some respects I had.

Show you're meeting the audience's needs when you ask for questions

You can also make your audience feel you're addressing their needs directly when you ask for questions. When you invite them to pose questions related to the topic just covered, you can ask, specifically, "What do you think about that solution I just gave you?" This encourages your listeners to articulate how they feel you've tailored your approach to them.

If they give you a positive response, acknowledge it with thanks. And if instead they say the solution doesn't work for them or they have some doubts, you have another opportunity to offer a suggestion that works for them and to make them feel the presentation is customized.

Customize your content wherever possible

If you have an anecdote that's generic, and you're addressing a particular group—sales executives, for example—edit the story if possible so it's a story about sales executives. When I talked to the deans, I told a story about a person whose responsibilities included disciplining his staff. As enforcers of the rules in their world, they could relate to this story. It made them feel as if I understood their roles because I told a story about others like themselves.

When I talk to people who are in a managerial capacity, I refer to other work I've done with C-level executives (CEOs, CFOs, etc.) to suggest that my presentation is tailored to people who, like them, are at the executive level.

When I taught the college students, I told a story about my own experience as a student making a presentation. That made them feel I understood who they were, and from the story they recognized how they could apply the techniques I taught in a college campus setting.

Give real-life uses they can relate to

Telling your audience what you're going to teach them is important, but to really get and keep their attention, you have to make them understand *why* they might need it.

One of my clients once told me, "I'm giving the audience information. They can figure out how to apply it." When I disputed that, he said, "I can't give them an example because I don't have one. This is an audience of project managers, and I've never presented to project managers."

The way you find examples is by talking to people like those who will be in your audience, doing research in advance, and mingling with the audience before the presentation. Mention your takeaways, and ask the person you're speaking to how they might be useful.

Half an hour before I spoke to a group of HR managers, I engaged one in conversation about three of the points I planned to cover. I asked if there were times she felt especially challenged by keeping her topic interesting. She said that happened during the meetings in which she was to help employees choose a health plan.

I also asked if she sometimes felt it difficult to stay on track. She cited presentations about sexual harassment, when the discussion often became heated and difficult to control.

Finally, I asked if making any specific presentations made her particularly nervous or fearful, and she said that happened when she had to address key objectives such as turnover and staffing.

This five-minute discussion directly before my presentation yielded gold. I took notes, and, after our talk, I spent another five minutes incorporating her examples under the appropriate tasks and subtasks on my blueprint.

When during my presentation I cited these examples, which the HR managers could apply in their world, I could see from their expressions they understood I was talking directly to them about things they could use, and they were rapt.

The most important way to tailor your approach to a particular audience is to give actual examples and demonstrate as clearly as possible how those examples apply to their situations. I cannot emphasize enough the importance of putting effort into this step. The payoff is enormous. You'll seem credible and empathic, and you'll find your audience much more attentive.

Your Turn to Tailor Your Approach

A generic presentation will be much more effective if your audience members feel that your material is meant specifically for them. Ideally, you can customize in advance, but you have to be prepared to do it in real time.

Review and exercises

Items flagged with arrows require action on your part. If you are uncertain how to proceed, reread the appropriate section in this chapter.

Edit in advance for specific audiences

▶ Customize takeaway hooks for the specific audience.

▶ Do additional research for the specific audience. Decide on the questions that can help you identify their pain points and pleasure points.

▶ Customize your title slide. Decide on the words you will use to identify your audience.

▶ Consider the sensibilities of the group you are addressing.

▶ Test out your material beforehand.

▶ Plan questions that are geared specifically to your audience.

▶ Determine the mood of the audience in advance if possible and be prepared to match it.

Spot the signs that your audience needs a spark

▶ Write in your own words how you can determine if you're losing the attention of your audience.

Create a smooth, customized presentation on the fly

▶ Create a *circle of knowledge* question you can ask that will elicit their needs.

▶ Write in your own words the various ways you can show empathy.

▶ Review how to give examples that show you are tailoring the material to them.

▶ Show your audience real-life applications of the material you are giving them. This requires advance preparation and brief interviews on the day of the presentation. Choose an appropriate takeaway from your agenda. Before the presentation, approach three audience members and ask each of them when or how they might need that skill. Incorporate those examples into your presentation.

Chapter Thirteen

STAY ON SCHEDULE

Deliver a presentation that ends on time, every time.

When I give a presentation that's scheduled to be an hour long, if I start at ten thirty, I end at eleven thirty. If I give a ten-minute presentation, I end exactly ten minutes later, and if I am supposed to deliver a four-hour presentation that starts at one o'clock, my audience can count on being able to walk out the door at five. A good presenter learns to do that.

I'm going to teach you how to calibrate your message so no matter what happens in your presentation, you can get it back on track.

To manage your pace:

- Create a timetable.
- Manage audience question periods.
- Adjust as you go.

186

Create a Timetable

The primary reason presenters have problems with pacing is they haven't done enough advance planning. Once you have prepared the blueprint for your presentation, you have to test it, adjust it, and document it.

I have advised that you should plan to cover four to eight agenda items in a one-hour presentation, and I have suggested that you should be able to deliver it in fifty minutes (the ten-minute gap is meant to leave time for questions).

Ideally, your practice run should hit the mark exactly. That is, it should take you fifty minutes for a scheduled one-hour presentation and an hour and forty minutes for a presentation that's scheduled for two hours. But when you do a trial run of your presentation for the first or second time, you'll probably find you're running short or long. This is why planning and practice are essential.

If your practice presentation is too long

Nearly half the time, you will discover the presentation you have created is running too long.

Speed up your speaking pace

It is possible you are simply speaking too slowly. Many presenters speak slowly because they think their audience will better understand what it is they have to say. To an extent, this is true. It's effective to speak slowly when you're covering something that's very important or that might be hard to understand. But if you speak too slowly, or speak slowly too often, you may bore your audience. If you haven't gone through the exercises in chapter 7 to ensure you are speaking at the appropriate presentation pace (between 150 and 180 words per minute), then do so now.

Cut out fillers

You may be surprised when I tell you the primary reason may not be that you are speaking too slowly or have too much to say, but that you are using too many words to say what you want to. Editors know that to improve anything you have written, the best place to start is by cutting it down.

Since you should be using a blueprint rather than a script, much of the editing you have to do is a matter of training yourself not to fall into certain speaking traps. If you haven't gone through the exercises for becoming aware of and eliminating filler words and phrases ("so," "and," "all right," and the others I described in chapter 7), then do so now.

Watch out for redundancies

Here's a transcription of a portion of a presentation about using computer software to book a camping tour: "You'll notice on the following slide, we actually have a picture of the key campsites you can visit. Now, as we mentioned, the campsites each have a description. When I select a campsite in my travel guide survey, it's going to display here as a description of the campsite. There is only one place where the description is going to show up, in the travel guide survey."

I suggested the presenter cut this to the bare minimum:

- Start with a directional: "Look at the slide."
- Make sure the audience members know what they are looking at: "Do you see *the travel guide survey*?" Pause.
- Explain the reason to look at it: "This is where the campsite description will show up." Pause.

Done.

Reducing the amount of dialogue not only makes the presentation shorter, but also ensures that your point doesn't get lost in a blizzard of words that may cause people to tune you out.

If your practice presentation is too short

A little more than half of the time, people discover that their presentation is too short. From your point of view, this is undesirable because you will not have made full use of the time allotted to you. From the audience's point of view, this is undesirable because you will have made them feel shortchanged.

Slow down your speaking pace

This is the most obvious place to start. Many presenters speak too quickly because they are afraid their audience will get bored and stop listening. Again, this is true only up to a certain point. If you speak too quickly, your audience may not be able to follow what you're saying. At minimum, they may feel you're glossing over the material, that the material isn't important, or that you're rushing for some reason.

If you haven't gone through the exercises described in chapter 7 for speaking at the appropriate presentation pace (between 150 and 180 words per minute), then do so now.

Give your listeners more time to absorb your message

If the problem is not that you are speaking too fast, it's easy to jump to the next conclusion: that you should add content. However, if you have planned your presentation carefully, adding content is unlikely to be a good solution. Once you have figured out what is essential to putting your message or idea across, padding your presentation will probably not make it better. It may even have the opposite effect of making it boring and repetitious.

You simply may not be allowing enough time for the audience to take in all the ideas you are presenting. I have mentioned the power of the pause before. Pausing after you have made a statement that is especially significant is very helpful in getting your audience to absorb and remember an essential idea. For example, when talking to people about making presentations, I might say, "Facial expressions are the only universal form of communication." Then I will pause and give the audience a couple of seconds to take that in before I continue.

You may even combine a pause with a directional. For example: "Audiences don't laugh because something's funny." (Pause.) "They laugh because they're feeling good." (Pause again. Insert directional.) "Think about that." (Pause again.) (Find more ideas for directionals in chapters 6 and 10.)

Ask the audience more questions

Review the exercises in chapter 10 for asking different types of questions. To add more time to your presentation, simply change a statement you would normally make into a question to ask your audience. The response and interaction with your audience members will not only add time but also keep them more engaged.

For example, instead of saying, "That process will save you time in your next job," you could say, "How might that process save you time in your next job?" Even a simple pause from you, with no response from your audience, will add a few seconds to your presentation and create the added benefit of stimulating your audience to consider how what you're offering might benefit them.

Add an agree and see if you're right *to your blueprint*

To add even more time, introduce another *agree and see if you're right*. This will not only give you the benefit of interaction and more engagement with the audience but also add another one or two minutes while the teams have a discussion and then relay their answers to you.

Or try another version of *agree and see if you're right*. After you've made an interesting point, ask, "Why do you think this is so?" (which is a leading question) and immediately add, "Take thirty seconds and agree with the person next to you on an answer."

Document the timing

This is a critical step. Once you have sped up or slowed down your presentation so it's the correct length, practice that version three times. During the third run-through, make a note of how many minutes into the presentation you should be introducing each takeaway in order to end on schedule.

Transfer this information into your blueprint so you will have guidelines to follow when you are actually making your presentation. If you are scheduled to begin your one-hour presentation at three o'clock, and based on your rehearsals you know that to stay on schedule you have to introduce the first takeaway at ten minutes past the hour, note 3:10 in the margin of your blueprint. If the next takeaway should come up at about 3:21, note that, too, in the margin, and so on.

Those markers will be invaluable when you are actually giving your presentation.

Manage Audience Question Periods

Faulty planning is the number one cause of pace problems. The best way to resolve these problems is by managing questions that come from the audience.

It is essential that you build question periods into your planning. Imagine shopping for a car. The salesman is discussing its features and terms, but when you ask a question, he says, "You can't ask any questions until I've finished what I plan to say." You'd go to a different car dealer. Why? Because you feel this one isn't meeting your needs. Similarly, you will lose your audience if you don't respond to their questions in a timely manner.

Answering questions may benefit you as well as the audience members. A question may give you an opportunity to provide a fuller explanation of one of your points. This may make your presentation more helpful to the audience and more successful for you.

Generally, presenters tell the audience to hold questions when they're afraid they will run out of time before they've finished. If you plan properly, this won't happen. In fact, you can use questions to *make sure* you finish on time.

Build question periods into your blueprint

I recommend building in ten minutes of question time per hour, allowing about five minutes for questions during the presentation and five minutes at the end. You may be unaccustomed to getting that many questions, but that will change if you improve your presentation. If people care about your topic and are engaged by your presentation, they will ask questions. (In the next chapter, I'll show you how to ensure you'll get some.)

Building in these ten-minute question sessions has the extra benefit of giving you flexibility if your presentation is running long or short.

Divide the five minutes of questions during the presentation into three intervals—one at the end of every other takeaway, just before you introduce the next. Make a note on your blueprint to remind yourself to ask for questions.

Questions fall into two categories:

- *In-scope questions* are relevant to whatever is being discussed, and the answers will be relevant to everyone.
- *Out-of-scope questions* may be completely irrelevant or they may apply only to a very limited number of people and possibly only to the questioner.

Encourage in-scope question to slow down pace

If you find your presentations are often ending too early, you may not be getting enough questions. Though I will give you some additional techniques to prompt questions in chapter 14, the place to start is by asking for question the right way. The way you ask dramatically affects the number of questions you get.

People are often uncomfortable about asking a question. How many times have you heard people say, "I can't believe I'm asking this, it's so stupid, but . . ."? You can see why it is a mistake to ask (as many presenters do), "Do you have any questions?" To many people, that is like saying, "Is anybody not really smart here? Is there anyone who doesn't get it? In fact, raise your hand right now so everyone in the room will know for sure you don't get it."

Phrase your inquiry another way. Instead of saying, "Do you have any questions?," say, "What questions do you have about [whatever it was you just taught]?" Here's why that's powerful:

- You've implied you *expect* questions, so people won't feel foolish about asking one. They'll feel safe about asking a question, and feeling safe is important to your audience. When they feel safe, they'll ask more questions, which will help ensure you have enough content.
- You've directed people's focus to thinking about what question they are going to ask. This will elicit quicker responses, which also helps manage your pace.
- By asking what questions people might have about the topic you've just covered, you've guided them to ask questions you're well prepared to answer. This bolsters your credibility and ensures you don't waste time answering out-of-scope questions.

Someone who attended one of my presentations said I seemed to know in advance what people would ask.

"I did know," I said. He was taken aback. I explained I had told the people in the audience what I wanted them to ask. I didn't simply ask for questions. I specifically said, "What are your questions about [topic]?" I had all my answers ready.

"What if the question was about a topic you weren't prepared for?" he asked.

"I'd have said, 'I'll answer that right before we're scheduled to end.'" And I would have employed some of the techniques I'll describe in chapter 14.

Postpone out-of-scope questions to speed up pace

Even if you invite only in-scope questions that relate to the agenda item(s) you've just finished covering by saying, "What questions do you have about [topic]?," people may still ask you out-of-scope questions. Answering them is likely to slow you down. If you want to stay on schedule, postpone the out-of-scope questions. (More on this in chapter 14.)

Adjust as You Go

Make sure your presentation is going according to your timetable, but never let the audience catch you checking the time. You don't want to give the impression you aren't interested in being responsive to them.

Before your presentation, check out the room where you'll speak. Ideally, there will be a clock at the back of the room, so if you glance at it you'll simply appear to be looking at the audience. If there's no clock, take off your watch and put it next to your blueprint. To check the time, you'll only have to glance downward momentarily.

In the margins of your blueprint you should have noted the exact time you should begin to cover each agenda item. Suppose at 3:30 you begin a topic and see from your margin note you weren't supposed to be at this point until 3:21. Or, suppose it's 3:21 and your margin note indicates you were supposed to be here at 3:30.

The first thing to do is . . . nothing. That is, try not to react. The audience has a sixth sense. People can often detect when you're anxious or something's wrong, which will make them uneasy and likely to lose focus. Avoid any change of facial expression that might reveal your feelings, and do your best to convey calm with your body language: stand still and keep your hands to your sides (or, alternatively for women, loosely clasped in front of you). Don't pace, move around, or fidget. Keep your pace and volume normal and your inflection even.

Under no circumstances say, "We're running out of time," or "We have extra time." If you've planned well, you have chosen as your last topic one that is especially compelling. You may even have intrigued some members of your audience enough to sit through your four-hour presentation especially to hear the last ten minutes. If you say (or even imply) you're running out of time and may have to skip the last topic, or even if you rush to cover everything, no matter how good your presentation has been to that point, you will lose those people.

Fortunately, you are constantly able to track your pace because your agenda is on the PowerPoint slide and the blueprint. Every time you click to a new slide and you see a new takeaway to discuss, by looking at your blueprint you can check whether or not you're hitting your marks.

If you check your blueprint regularly, you can stay on track without having to lop off or add a huge amount of time all in one spot. Instead, you can make subtle adjustments.

If you're running behind schedule

You have a couple of options to speed things up in real time.

Speed up your pace

If you discover at your first or second takeaway you're running long, immediately begin to shave a minute or two off each of the subsequent takeaways and see if you can get back on track. It is better to make adjustments as you go than to postpone your cuts; the later you begin to trim, the more drastically your presentation will be affected. Once you have some experience, you will get better at doing minor cutting here and there without getting anxious and catching the audience's attention.

Or you can rely on the easiest, quickest fix of all.

Invite fewer questions

Normally, I recommend you ask for questions every other takeaway. However, if you realize there is not enough time when you are at one of your pace markers, cut down. If you have an hour-long presentation with six takeaways, instead of inviting questions after the second and fourth, invite them only after the third. Or eliminate them entirely. Then, if there's time, you can invite questions at the end (after takeaway 6).

Incidentally, this is an argument against using a slide that says "Questions," because you can't simply omit the question period without the audience noticing. Analytic presenters do like to work with a questions slide, but I strongly suggest just making a note on your blueprint page at the appropriate spot.

If you're running ahead of schedule

There are a few ways you can slow down your presentation in real time.

Slow down your pace

Once you find out you're ahead of schedule, add a minute or two to each of the agenda items that follow. Again, be sure to do this by checking your markers early in the presentation so that your presentation is less dramatically affected and you do not have to figure out how to add a whole lot at the end. Once you have some experience, you can do this without getting anxious and without the audience noticing.

Add a directional
Say, "Write that down" periodically. The learners who need to write things down in order to absorb them will do so and that will buy you time.

Add an **agree and see if you're right**
Simply transform one or more of the leading questions from your blueprint into an *agree and see if you're right*. For example, if you would normally ask your audience what effect they think marketing has on sales, instead tell them to take thirty seconds to write down their opinion and another thirty seconds to agree with the person next to them. Then re-ask them the question. You just added a minute or two to your presentation.

Invite more questions
In addition to asking for questions at every other takeaway, when you're running short ask for them at every takeaway—and even, if necessary, every sub-takeaway. For example, if the content of this chapter were one of your topics, in addition to asking "What questions do you have about pace?," you could also ask, "What questions do you have about timing your presentation?" and "What questions do you have about watching the clock?" and "What questions do you have about managing questions?"

If you have created a blueprint with multiple agenda points, adding or subtracting just a minute or two from each will permit you to get back on track.

Your Turn to Stay on Schedule
An audience gets fidgety if you run past the scheduled time and feels shortchanged if you end too soon. Ending right on time makes you look credible and professional.

Review and exercises
Items flagged with arrows require action on your part. If you are uncertain how to proceed, reread the appropriate section in this chapter.

Create a timetable
▶ Time a practice run.

▶ If your practice presentation is too long, determine where you might use any of these remedies:

- Speed up your pace.
- Cut down on fillers.
- Trim redundancies.

▶ If your practice presentation is too short, determine where you might use any of these remedies:

- Slow down your pace (see also chapter 7).
- Add pauses.
- Ask more questions (see also chapter 10).
- Add an *agree and see if you're right*.

▶ Document your timing: Once it is established, make note of times in your blueprint margins to indicate at what time you should start each takeaway.

Manage audience question periods

▶ Build question periods into your blueprint: Decide on the words you'll use to tell your audience what kinds of questions you will take.

Adjust as you go

▶ Plan how you will check the time as you go.

▶ Make sure times to begin each takeaway are noted in the margins.

If you need to slow your pace:

▶ Decide on the words you will use to encourage in-scope questions.

If you need to speed up your pace:

▶ Decide on the words you will use to limit out-of-scope questions.

If you're off schedule:

▶ Write in your own words the procedures you will follow if you are running behind.

▶ Write in your own words the procedures you will follow if you are running ahead of schedule.

Chapter Fourteen

ANSWER ANY QUESTION

Elicit questions and provide answers even when you have none

If you handle questions well, you meet your audience's needs, which earns you credibility and respect; you keep the audience focused and engaged, and you look like a pro.

I taught a new employee in her early twenties some of the techniques for handling questions that are described in this chapter. Soon afterward, she presented to a group of customers for eight hours, and then she took them on a tour of her company.

The company has a "wall of hands," a montage of plaster impressions of the hands of its employees. When you've been with the firm for ten years, the company adds your hand impression to the wall. When the young woman brought the group to the wall, they asked where hers was displayed. She'd been with the company just four months, but because she was so skillful at handling questions, they assumed she was a veteran.

Handling questions is a matter of mastering how to:

- Elicit questions from the audience.
- Answer in-scope questions immediately.
- Cope confidently when you don't know the answer.
- Postpone out-of-scope questions gracefully.

Elicit Questions from the Audience

Questions are a sign people are interested and provide an opportunity for interaction that makes your presentation livelier. Presenters often tell me they have a hard time getting responses when they invite questions. You can turn that around with just a few simple techniques.

Make people feel safe to ask a question

Adult learners' greatest fear is looking foolish in front of their peers. That's why, as I've mentioned, if you ask, "Do you have any questions?," chances are you'll get nothing but dead silence. No one wants to be the first to raise a hand for fear of looking as if he or she is the sole individual in the room who doesn't understand what's going on.

If instead you say, "What questions do you have about [the topic you've just covered]?," you've increased the likelihood of a response. You've suggested that you fully expect there will be questions, and therefore no one should be embarrassed to ask one. Still, you will have to wait for one to come.

Wait seven seconds to get a response

The real key to getting questions is taking enough time to wait for them. Typically, presenters invite questions, wait a beat or so, say, "Then let's continue," and go immediately to the next topic. When I point this out after an observation, the usual response is, "Nobody spoke up, and I felt so awkward and weird standing there silently while they stared at me, so I figured I should just move on."

But you have to wait. You have to wait a full seven seconds. Though that's not a lot of time, it can feel like an eternity. Do it anyway.

Here's why: The average human being needs one or two seconds to process a question, another three or four to come up with a response, and one to two more to get the courage up to ask the question publicly.

And though you may find the wait uncomfortable, I'll remind you (yes, again) that this presentation is not about you; it's about your audience. You may experience discomfort while you're waiting, but they won't. You may feel they're looking at you, but in fact, they're not paying any attention to you. They're thinking about what you just asked. While you're waiting, their brains are busy.

You will be more comfortable if you use the techniques I described to display confidence, taking the stance I have previously described. Swivel your head slowly from one side of the room to the other, gazing across the entire audience, so everyone knows you're just waiting for a question. The more calm and confident you look, the more questions you're apt to get.

The first question often arrives just before the seventh second. If you allow less time, you may not get any questions at all.

Answer In-Scope Questions Immediately

I explained in chapter 13 that to manage your pace, you establish boundaries and tell your audience you will be answering only questions related to the topic during the question period but will postpone others until the end of the presentation.

If you expect to be bombarded by questions, you may want to establish these boundaries after the introduction and the *circle of knowledge* and before the first topic. (Make a note to yourself on the blueprint to do so.) Say, "I'm going to answer every one of your questions. Any question that is specifically about the topic I'm covering at the moment and relates to everyone, I'll answer right away. I'll answer any other questions right before the close of the presentation for you and others who might be interested."

If the presentation is longer than an hour, I recommend distributing a handout I call "My Questions" along with the agenda handout. Tell people to write down any unanswered questions on the sheet and say you'll answer them five minutes before each break or right before the close of the presentation for those who might be interested.

This boundary sets the stage for the audience so that when you apply the techniques in this chapter, they will be prepared and even encouraged by your follow-through.

Show you care

The way you respond to the question is not nearly as important as how you respond to the questioner. You need to show that person that you care, that you will meet his or her need, and that you know the answer.

Caring and meeting the need are as important as showing you know the answer. I have watched many sales and technical professionals, trainers, executives, and other kinds of presenters take a question but ignore the person who is asking it. Some of them even appear to be annoyed someone would bother them with a question. I don't understand that. Your goal is to give the impression that hearing a question from someone in your audience is the most important thing you could be doing at the moment.

However, though you are about to focus on the individual who is asking a question, be sure to keep your connection to the audience as a whole. That is, keep your feet angled to include as much of the audience as possible, not pointed exclusively toward the speaker. Your body language should say, *Hey, everybody, I'm still thinking about all of you. I'm going to give this person the floor for a few seconds but I still care about* everyone *in the room.*

And then make one-on-one contact with your questioner. Tilt your head slightly toward the person, referring to him or her by name if you can, and say, "What's your question?"

Be a responsive listener

Look the questioner right in the eye

This is the only occasion in your entire presentation when you make direct eye contact with a single individual for longer than a second or two. Stay focused as long as the person is speaking.

Stay put

Remain in the sweet spot. Walking toward the speaker will be intimidating. Walking away will make you look as if you're in retreat and signal you don't know the answer.

Nod subtly, and use reflective words and phrases

Men may have to make more of a conscious effort to do this than women. As linguist Lynette Hirschman has pointed out, women tend to make "listening noises" when another person is speaking—noises such as "mm-hm," "uh-huh," "I see," and "okay"—as a way of signaling *I'm hearing you*. Men are more are likely to give silent attention.

Because women expect those listening noises, they may interpret silent attention as inattention. Men, on the other hand, may incorrectly interpret listener noises as signals the listener agrees with what's being said. But generally, people recognize the noises are reassurances that mean, *I'm listening and I get what you're saying*.

Paraphrase the question

When the person has finished speaking, paraphrase the question so the questioner (and the audience) knows you understood it perfectly.

There are several ways to handle a paraphrase. Here are some examples:

- "It sounds as if you want to know . . ."
- "I want to make sure I understand your question . . ."
- "I want to make sure we're using the proper terminology . . ."
- "Are you referring to . . . ?"
- "Let me make sure I have this right . . ."
- "Ah, you're asking about . . ."
- "Oh, you're wondering . . ."
- "So, you want to know . . . ?"

You can even expand the original statement when you paraphrase. If someone says, "Is cheese and beer all that Wisconsin is known for?," you can say, "It sounds as if you're asking what Wisconsin is known for around the country in terms of food and drink. Is that right?"

People I coach often balk at the idea of paraphrasing questions, but it's necessary. It serves several purposes:

- It ensures that everyone in the room hears the question.
- It helps the questioner make sure the question really gets at what he or she wants to know. When you paraphrase, the person may realize it's necessary to restate the question.

- It helps you be certain you interpret the question accurately. This not only saves time but also saves face for you. Many times I hear someone say, "That's a great answer. But I asked a different question."
- It gives you a neutral way to respond to every question whether or not you know the answer, so the audience can't tell the difference.
- It buys you time to decide whether to answer the question now or to postpone it because it is not of general interest or because you need time to figure out the answer.
- And the number one reason: It proves you've really been listening and you care about the person.

Questioners who are satisfied with the way you've paraphrased the question will feel their needs will be met because you understand their concerns. If they aren't satisfied, they will at least feel your concern when you listen as they attempt to restate the question and then you try to paraphrase it.

The whole process—the asking of the questions and the paraphrase—should last for fifteen to thirty seconds and no more. After that, take your attention away from the individual and direct it back where it belongs, to the audience as a whole.

Answer in-scope questions immediately

When I ask presenters how they decide whether or not they'll answer a question, nine out of ten say it depends on whether or not they know the answer. But remember—the presentation is about the audience, not about you. Your decision should be based on one concern only: Is the question in scope?

In-scope questions are directly related to the topic and nearly everyone in the room needs an immediate answer. These questions must be answered right away. Out-of-scope questions need not be.

Novice presenters are sometimes frightened by the prospect of knowing the answer to every question. They tell me, "I don't know all the content I'm supposed to know. I'd have to prepare for ten more years to get it all." That's not so. If you follow the ground rules I have suggested and answer only the in-scope questions, you will be much more likely to know the answers, and I'll give you a technique to handle those you don't.

Deliver your answer with maximum impact

I have said the only time you make eye contact for an extended period of time with a single individual is when you are listening to that person's question. When you are answering, use the stance and eye contact techniques that include the entire audience. You may glance back to the asker in this case, but for the most part, include the entire audience just as if you were in presentation mode.

Pull drifters back in

Many people tune out when they hear someone ask a question they think doesn't apply to them. They hunch over their laptops, surf the Internet, check their email, or simply allow their minds to wander. When you're asked an in-scope question, you want to pull those people back to the presentation to make sure they hear your answer. After you paraphrase the question, here are some of the things you might say to do that:

- "What Joe is asking is very important."
- "Joe raises a question that affects everyone in the room."
- "Take a look up here."
- "To answer that question, let's review."
- "Who can relate to that?"
- "I'll bet others need clarification, too."

Once you've given your answer, if the person who asked the question is nodding and looking satisfied, or making notes—in other words, if the person is clearly responding positively and attentively to your comments—look over and say, "Did that help?," and you'll likely hear, "Yes it did. Thank you."

If your questioner looks upset or puzzled, you don't want to lose your credibility, so just move on and approach him later to settle things.

Stay on track after the question

If you have spare time after you've answered any questions, you might prompt more. Ask, "What other questions do you have about [topic]?" as a gesture to show you care and elicit more responses.

When you run out of time for a question period, simply move on to the next topic. Use a directional to refocus their attention. Say, "Take a look up here" and indicate the agenda on your PowerPoint and then introduce the next takeaway: "Next, I'm going to show you how to . . ."

Cope Confidently When You Don't Know the Answer

In the unlikely event you've forgotten or don't know the answer to an in-scope question, be cautious. Audiences have an uncanny knack for spotting a presenter's weakness.

Don't telegraph the fact that you don't know by doing any of the following. Each is a sure giveaway you are stumped:

- *Asking "Could you repeat the question, please?"* Ding-ding-ding-ding-ding! Alarm bells immediately go off in audience's heads. They recognize the speaker doesn't know the answer because the speaker was able to answer all the previous questions right off the bat.
- *Looking up or down or to the side*—or anywhere other than at the audience.
- *Walking or taking a step backward.*
- *Saying, "Good question."* If some audience members feel the question is irrelevant, your praise may reflect badly on you. Or, if you indicate one question is good, you may be expected to comment positively all of them. And finally, that response suggests you know the answer; if that proves not to be so, that puts you in a poor light. I suggest instead you periodically say, "Thank you for that question." It conveys appreciation, which pleases everyone; suggests nothing about whether or not you know the answer; and seems gracious, particularly if you are going to postpone the answer.

Most presenters deny doing any of these things, but they're very common, even among the deniers.

Professional card players search for the subtle change of expression that reveals what's in the other player's mind. They try to maintain what's known as a poker face—one that's hard to read because it doesn't betray any emotion. Try to keep a poker face in this situation, avoid the behaviors I have described, and go through the same motions in response to every question, regardless of whether you know the answer or not.

Limit saying "I don't know"

You may be asked some in-scope questions you aren't able to answer. You can simply say, "I don't know the answer," and add, "I'll get back to you at the end of the session." Be sure to give an exact time. This is a perfectly valid response and, in many venues, the right one.

However, my research has shown you get only three "get out of jail free" cards with your audience. When you say you don't know more than three times, you can lose your credibility. Here's an alternative solution:

- Start with: "I have a few thoughts about that, but I want to make sure I get the exact answer you're looking for." This shows you care and want to meet the need of the asker.
- Next, say, "Go ahead and write that down." That's inviting and actionable. Also if the questioner is occupied with writing, he or she is not arguing with you about not getting the answer immediately!
- Finally, say, "I'll have an answer for you by the end of the session."

You're telling the truth: You have a few thoughts. You've said you'll meet a need by giving the person the exact answer. You've told that person to write it down, which keeps him or her busy and not focused on what you don't know. You've promised an answer at a specific time. And you haven't said you don't know the answer.

Be sure to follow up on these questions. When the audience sees you follow up, you will have delivered on a promise, so you enhance your credibility and ensure they believe you and your future responses.

Keep in mind you only get three "get out of jail free" cards. That is, if during your presentation you say, "I don't know" (or even suggest it, in some fashion) to an in-scope question more than three times, you can appear inexperienced and not credible.

Let me reassure you that if you know your content, it is very unlikely you will ever get more than three in-scope questions you can't answer. Out-of-scope questions are another matter. Here's how to make your "get out of jail free" problem go away.

Postpone Out-of-Scope Questions Gracefully

When you get a question that is not directly relevant to the material at hand, treat it like any question—*whether or not you know the answer*. First paraphrase it and thank the questioner. Then add, "Tell you what. Write that down, and let's talk about that at [give a specific time, depending on when the break will come], you and I," adding, ". . . and anyone else who might like to join us," if you think others might be interested.

With that response, you've achieved all of the following:

- "Let's" is an inviting phrase and shows the questioner you care.
- Questioners will know you're going to meet their needs because you told them to write down the question and indicated when you would answer it. Giving such individual attention sets you apart from other presenters.
- You've followed through on your question boundary, which shows your audience you keep your promises.
- You haven't suggested you don't know the answer (even if you don't).
- You don't waste the time of the majority of the audience answering a question they didn't come to hear.
- You'll be able to manage your pace much more effectively because you won't get numerous out-of-scope questions.

If the questioner looks as if he or she is good with this plan, get acknowledgment by saying, "Is this okay with you?" Most likely you'll get a response such as, "Sure, that'll be fine," and then everyone will be aware of how you're building rapport. If a questioner doesn't seem satisfied, move on, and handle that person one-on-one at a break. The person may be among the chronically difficult types (such as Resenters, Hecklers, and Experts), whom I'll help you deal with in the next chapter.

If it's possible, use the break time to search the Internet, send an email, or make a phone call to find the answers you're missing. If you get one, great; but if you can't, at the end of the session speak to the questioner and say, "You know, I don't have the answer to this, but I'm going to take your email address, and I'll get the answer to you by the end of the week." He's the only one who'll know you don't have the answer at your fingertips, and what will matter more to him is you're meeting his needs.

Respond to all questions by the end of the presentation

Even if you don't have a final answer, I believe you have an obligation to take care of the people in your audience by making sure you have responded to every question. Joe may have flown cross-country for your presentation, and the question he wants to ask may be the one thing he wanted to get out of it. But you can't slow down the entire presentation to meet the immediate needs of a single individual.

Sticking to your boundaries will help you as well as your audience. If you answer just one out-of-scope question—or even (be warned!) just a small portion of that question—you'll get more questions like it. But if you postpone effectively, people will ask fewer questions of this type, and you'll probably have only three to six left to answer at the end of an hour-long presentation.

Make your summary five minutes before you are scheduled to end (". . . And you have just learned five strategies to create new sources of income with less risk"), then pause, look at your audience, and conclude by asking for questions about the entire presentation ("What questions do you have about increasing business with new low-risk loans?").

Then put up your final slide, offering, "Those of you who have additional questions, stick around," express your thanks, and close with a pleasantry (see chapter 16).

Stay front and center as people leave, showing you're ready to hang out and answer questions from people who want to stay. Don't sit down and don't talk to somebody in a corner, or others will think you're not there for them. Remember, there are questions you promised earlier to answer, so it's time to follow through on your promise. This will build trust for future presentations with this audience.

Often, 15 percent or less of the audience will stay to discuss the extra questions. This indicates 85 percent or more wouldn't have been that interested in the answers anyway. But by extending the invitation to stay, you made all the audience members feel you wanted to meet their needs.

The answers to their questions often matter to people far less than getting their needs met. Constantly reinforcing the message that you will meet their needs and being certain to follow through will help make you an outstanding presenter.

Your Turn to Answer Any Question

Having the ability to respond to every question—whether or not you know the answer—makes you seem like a pro, and taking the time to respond to every question makes you seem credible and empathic.

Review and exercises

Items flagged with arrows require action on your part. If you are uncertain how to proceed, reread the appropriate section in this chapter.

Elicit questions from the audience

▶ Decide what words you will use to make people feel safe when you ask for a question.

▶ How long should you wait for a response?

Answer in-scope questions immediately

▶ Decide on the words you will use to establish boundaries.

▶ Determine when in the presentation you will make that statement.

▶ Review how to handle questions if the presentation lasts more than an hour.

▶ Write in your own words how to include the entire audience while you are answering a question.

▶ Write in your own words what body language you should use when you are answering a question.

▶ Decide on the words you will use to call on a questioner.

▶ Decide on the words you will use to introduce your paraphrase of a question.

▶ Decide on the words you will use to pull drifters back in.

▶ Decide on the words you will use when you run out of time in a question period.

▶ Decide on the words you will use to move out of the question period.

Cope confidently even when you don't know the answer

▶ Write in your own words the behaviors that telegraph the fact you do not know an answer.

► Decide on the words will use when you don't know an answer.

► Write the steps to take when you get a question you can't answer.

Postpone out-of-scope questions gracefully

► Decide on the words you will use to postpone a question.

► Decide on the words you will use to get the questioner to acknowledge your plan.

► Write what you will do if you don't get acknowledgment.

► Decide when and with what words you will invite final in-scope questions.

► Decide when and with what words you will ask for any unanswered questions.

Practice answering questions

► Have a practice session with a colleague. Make a list of ten questions: three in scope to which you know the answer, three in scope to which you don't know the answer, and four out of scope. Then, ask each other the ten questions, practicing the above techniques. Remember to use the right body language and tone.

Chapter Fifteen

MINIMIZE DISTRACTIONS

Remain in charge no matter what's happening

Eventually, every presenter has to deal with distractions caused by misbehaving audience members.

Educational psychologist Rudolf Dreikurs suggested that misbehavior is caused by people who don't feel they belong. They may resort to disruptive behavior, seeking attention and power so they'll be included; they may seek revenge to get back at the organization or people they resent; or they may become apathetic, feeling the situation is hopeless.

I have developed practical solutions that allow you to handle such problems quickly and easily, staying in charge without being heavy-handed.

You'll learn how to:

- Stop interruptions.
- Handle negativity.
- Manage inattention.

Stop Interruptions

People may stop the flow of your presentation by jumping in with questions and comments or trying to start conversations at inappropriate times. Their motives may not be negative. Some are what I have described as Talk Learners who are simply trying to absorb what you're saying. They're talking aloud while you deliver your message because they need to say it to get it.

When you ask questions throughout the presentation, these people often respond mentally and sometimes aloud as well, even without being called on (and even if your question is purely rhetorical). Including the *circle of knowledge* and *agree and see if you're right* techniques, which give them a managed opportunity to talk, can be helpful. Still, the Talk Learners don't pose major problems.

The major problems come from the people who want the attention, power, or satisfaction of being publicly recognized. These Talk Hogs fall into two categories—the Expert, who actually has some information and credentials (but may want to challenge you), and the Know-It-Alls, who just want the spotlight. Both can take over a conversation and even overshadow your message, but only if you let them.

There are three very effective ways to deal with distractions from people who are seeking attention and power.

Reward only positive behavior

When I took my four-year-old nephew, Cole, to the grocery store, his father warned me, "He's going to ask you for a candy bar, but he is not allowed to eat candy bars during the trip to the store. He can have either a granola bar or a fruit snack." I thought being able to give my nephew choices would work out just great.

No sooner did we get to the store than Cole began tugging on my belt: "Uncle Jason, Uncle Jason, I want a candy bar." I knew once I made eye contact when he tugged, he would learn a powerful but negative lesson—that tugging and nagging would get him the attention he wanted.

If on the other hand I made eye contact only when he was behaving well and then said, "Hey, Cole, let's get you a granola bar or a fruit snack," he would learn he would get attention, and perhaps even a treat, only for good behavior.

It's important you invite dialogue, but it's also important you discourage your audience from interrupting at inappropriate times. Use the same technique

I used on Cole, ignoring them when they are engaging in bad behavior but giving them attention when their behavior is appropriate.

Talk Hogs really need attention, and they absolutely will find a way to get it, even, if necessary, with bad behavior. The key is to work with that need: feed it when they are behaving appropriately and ignore them when they're not. They'll get the message quickly.

Give the Experts the spotlight

In a small group, I often ask people to introduce themselves, and if someone seems very determined to make others aware of his or her specialty or the fact that she or he is a top-tier executive, I put an E (for Expert) next to that person's name on my seating chart.

Like any audience, but probably in greater proportion, such a group may include some people who want control and will attempt to take it if it's not given. One of my mentors once told me, "Jason, if you don't give your audience some control, they *will* take it from you." The secret is not to relinquish control but instead to share it with them.

Acknowledging their expertise is an excellent tactic. Say something like, "Joe, as a CFO, how would you handle this?" or "Joe, based on your expertise, where would you say is the starting point?" (Be sure to ask this kind of question only to someone with the authority or experience to answer, and ask the person directly, so that the Know-It-Alls don't jump in and try to respond.) Once you share control, the Expert is less likely to try to seize it.

I was ninety minutes into a presentation to a group of physicians when one arrived late, sat down, and, within minutes, interrupted to say what I was teaching wouldn't work for her and, what's more, was irrelevant. I didn't respond, so as not to reward bad behavior.

Only when she quieted down did I make eye contact with her to acknowledge her presence and the fact that she was listening. Then, as soon as I had the chance to ask a question in her specialty, I directed it to her. "What would you say is the most important thing to stress here?" Once I had turned the room over to her, even briefly, and she could deliver her expert answer correctly in front of her peers, she had her moment of glory. Afterward, she was off my case.

On another occasion, an executive in my presentation group made an obvious point of mentioning his title when he introduced himself. He was one of the most highly respected managers I've ever worked with, but his self-important attitude made me think he might be an Expert. I decided to be proactive rather than reactive and sought out his opinions at early and regular opportunities. Giving him a chance to shine prevented potential confrontation; it turned him into an ally rather than a competitor for attention.

Offer a one-on-one meeting

During one presentation, a consultant answered every question before I had a chance to respond. So I asked to speak with her briefly during the break. I acknowledged she was very well informed but explained I was having difficulty getting my message across when she interrupted with her answers.

She wasn't a complete Expert (her answers were often wrong); she was simply a Know-It-All. But by singling her out during the break, I gave her the attention she craved. I suggested perhaps I could give her a little signal whenever I needed her to hold off on a comment and give me some time. We agreed that when that happened, I could simply put my hand on the table. That's all it took to solve the problem.

Handle Negativity

Negative people tend to be Resenters, Naysayers, or Faultfinders.

It's important to understand the motivation of such people who are at a presentation. They are often people who were required to attend, and they resent it. They come with an attitude that is not conducive to learning or to useful dialogue.

Rudolf Dreikurs would say their misbehavior is just the manifestation of desire for revenge, misdirected at the presenter rather than toward whoever required his or her presence.

Nip a power struggle in the bud

Simply relinquishing some control to a Naysayer—someone who either makes a comment or whose expression reveals he or she is unhappy to be there—can sometimes resolve a problem quickly. The key when you do that is to remain neutral, so the Naysayer doesn't focus on you but on the problem at hand.

Remember Cole's behavior in the grocery store? When he asked for a candy bar, I offered a fruit snack or a granola bar. By offering choices I was offering to share control, so I thought he'd choose and we'd move on.

Nope. He said, "I don't want those. I want a candy bar," and when I offered choices again, he tried a power struggle. He wanted me to argue and engage so he could argue back and win. He said, "Daddy would let me have one."

"Probably so," I said. Did I agree with him? Not quite. Did I disagree with him? Not really. I just sidestepped the argument. Cole looked at me and said, "You're the worst uncle ever." I wasn't letting him have his way and he wanted revenge.

It's not just kids who have tantrums. A fifty-year-old company veteran stood up in the middle of a presentation session introducing new techniques, said, "I refuse to learn this, and you can't make me," and exited. He resented having to be there and he wanted revenge.

A manager followed him to the corridor, where he continued to rant. "This is the worst presentation I've ever seen," he fumed. The manager responded perfectly: "Could be," she said. Then she offered a choice: "Do you want to stay and learn it today, or do you want me to send someone to your office to teach it to you tomorrow?"

The manager didn't argue; she avoided the struggle and offered a choice with limits. The situation resolved itself the same way mine and Cole's was resolved. After I'd said "probably so" and again offered choices, Cole realized the game was over. "Fruit snack," he said. Similarly, the angry company veteran finally agreed to return to the presentation.

To review:

- Say something neutral ("Could be") rather than disagree ("What?! The presenter is amazing!"). Since you're neither agreeing nor disagreeing, there's nothing to fight about.
- Nod your head and make listening noises to show you care what the person has to say.
- Offer a choice, in order to give the person back some control. When you give some power back to the Resenter, he or she is more apt to do what you want and less likely to be disruptive.

Establish a relationship with a Resenter

In another case, the presentation was for a company that was about to replace an old software program with a new one. All the employees were required to go for retraining. The presenter, with thirteen years of experience and a great reputation, entered the room where he would speak and was stunned to see the sign below taped to a computer monitor.

Figure 15.1. Sign of a Resenter.

The presenter had spent an entire weekend preparing for this presentation, which included twenty-four hours' worth of material. Then he walked in to discover this sign. Naturally, he was hurt. Typically, hurt turns into anger and often into a desire to retaliate. But when you're a presenter and the problem is someone in your audience, retaliation is impossible and also misguided. Again: it's not about you; it's about your audience.

The simple solution is to build rapport. Identify and meet with anyone in this category—before, during, or after the session—to find the person's goals and win him or her over. This trainer did that so successfully that afterward, the trainee actually wrote a letter of thanks to the organization for such a wonderful experience.

Waiting for the Resenter to cool down and hear him out required a great deal of patience from the trainer. He didn't betray any sense of being upset but requested a one-on-one meeting, asked about the Resenter's pain points and pleasure points, and listened carefully. Finally, he took the Resenter to lunch, listened some more, and paraphrased the Resenter's comments. He even wrote them all down.

When you initiate such a meeting, it's good to try for a light mood, but don't attempt humor. A Resenter is looking for revenge, and humor might not strike the right note. Instead, just listen. Remember, these people want revenge because they feel they don't have control. If you offer them solutions that involve choices, initially they might react negatively (like Cole, who persisted in wanting his candy bar). But if you stick to your guns, show you care, and keep offering choices, when they manage to get control of their emotions, they'll come around.

In this situation, the trainer's responsiveness made a huge impression on the trainee; no one before had ever given him the chance to express his needs, which had to do with feeling competent and skilled at his job. The trainer listened and then tried to meet as many of them as he could over the next three presentation days, pointing out how the new software could be easily learned and would make him more effective.

There's a scientific reason for dealing with anger this way. It's based on the idea of the three-part brain, a theory supported by respected scientists, including Carl Sagan:

- One part is the primitive reptilian brain, which controls instinctive behavior like aggression.
- Another is the paleomammalian complex, which developed in early mammals and handles the motivation and emotions connected to eating, reproduction, parenting, and other behaviors.
- And the third is the neocortex, or cerebral cortex (found only in mammals), which is responsible for planning and other abstractions.

The Resenters have to be acting unemotionally and processing information with their cerebral cortex before they can they make choices. Once you're aware of this, you won't take their tantrums personally. Working with them may take time but has a huge payoff.

Set ground rules with a Faultfinder

Faultfinders, another category of a negative person, come in two versions: Gripers and Hecklers. Dreikurs would probably say that all are feeling robbed of power. They are reluctant to try something new and doubt it will work as promised. Unlike the Research Learners, who tend to argue and debate to learn, the Faultfinders won't talk things through to a logical conclusion. Instead, they present a never-ending series of challenges and roadblocks.

A dead giveaway you're dealing with one of these people is when the phrase "Yeah, but" comes up a lot. The "yeah" is a lame attempt to placate you, and the "but" expresses total negativity.

I was beginning an all-day presentation to teach people how to use a certain type of software, and not five minutes had gone by when I'd already heard five or six gripes about it. I couldn't keep teaching in this situation. I knew what I had to do: I stopped and established ground rules.

When you set rules, you can't just talk about what you want; you have to offer something in return. I like to start with the phrase "tell you what," which sounds like a compromise to begin with. "Tell you what," I said. "It sounds like you all have a lot of issues with this software. For the next forty-five minutes, I'll listen to everything you have to say, and I'll write it all down.

"Then, I'll deliver all your comments to the people who make the decisions. I can't make any promises about what they will do, but I promise I'll take the comments to them." Notice that I didn't say I could guarantee results, but I could guarantee I would listen, which is the most appropriate response for what was really the underlying issue. The audience wanted the power of being heard.

"In return," I continued, "after that forty-five minutes, I would like you to give me the next six hours of your day so I can show you some amazing things you can take from this presentation to help in your life. Does that sound fair?" They agreed it was. So we had our ground rules and a win-win solution.

Don't think you'll never confront a similar situation. It may happen only occasionally, but you need to be prepared.

Turn the issue back to a Griper

People often gripe to gain power, and you give them the power briefly by asking what they would do. For example, whenever someone gripes ("I don't see how that's going to work," "I don't like these techniques"), ask the person how he or she would have handled the situation *without* the techniques you're presenting.

You're saying, in effect, *Take a moment, come up here on stage, stand up on the podium, and I'll move to the side. You'll have your chance to look good in front of all your peers, and then you can go back and sit down and leave me alone,* and that's exactly how it goes down.

Once he or she has gotten a power fix, the person is done. Remember, if you don't share control with your audience, they will take it from you. I let people who need it have their moment even if I don't agree with them, because that's what they need.

You often get some inadvertently amusing responses. People will offer a solution that turns out to be exactly what I suggested, in which case I say, "That sounds good. Why don't you do that?" Or they'll dig themselves into a hole, proposing something that, even as they speak, they realize won't work.

Sometimes they'll offer a solution that has worked really well for them in the past, and you can say to them, "We can work with that idea." Not only do they feel powerful as an expert sharing an idea, but the very exchange of this idea and your response turns you into teammates now rather than competitors, and often their guard will come down and their attitude will change from counterproductive to helpful.

Either way, the Gripers end up going exactly to the place I planned to take them, though they may never admit this is the case. Here's a typical exchange:

Griper: "Regarding what you said about how to handle questions: I would just simply listen to a question and then answer it."

You: "How does that work for you?"

Griper: "It works great. I don't need to postpone questions."

You: "It sounds like you don't get a lot of questions that are out of scope."

Griper: "No, I don't."

You: "Well, great, that works for you." It's over.

Don't give the Griper a second chance to express a complaint. You're enabling him or her rather than taking control of the situation.

Placate Hecklers

Hecklers are a combination of a Talk Hog and a Resenter. They often sit in the back of the room, making disparaging comments about the material or the presenter. Ironically, they often listen closely to the presentation in order to make their negative comment, so inattention isn't as much of an issue. But their disruptions end up distracting other audience members, so they need to be stopped.

Hecklers get their power and attention from putting others down. Handle them by ignoring their bad behavior when possible and, rather than get involved in a power struggle with them, give them options and not orders.

One of my favorite ways to do this for longer presentations is to offer the audience the choice of when they'd like to take a break. "Would you prefer a break now or in fifteen minutes?" Often, I'll even put it up for a vote. The vote keeps the audience engaged, and simultaneously offers power and control to the Heckler, even if it's only as part of a group.

Another way to share power with a Heckler and shut down his or her behavior is with a technique mentioned earlier in the chapter: asking questions that might draw on his or her expertise. I discussed asking a question of just one person, but you can also ask it of an Expert category that includes the Heckler.

For example, if you have a group that includes some financial professionals (and the Heckler is among them), you can ask, "Financial professionals in the room, what are some of the ways you have found effective to get buy-in on this type of loan?" The Heckler will often be among those who respond. Or one of his or her peers will answer, and when that happens, the Heckler will typically allow that person to have his moment. People rarely heckle those who share their expertise but tend to focus on the presenter or the presentation so that they can look good—that is, powerful—in front of those peers.

When the Heckler says something directly confrontational—perhaps you've made a suggestion and the Heckler says, "It wouldn't work"—do not acknowledge the comment with either eye contact or a statement. Let the moment pass, but address it subsequently, because silence indicates acceptance or approval. Respond only to indicate you heard the comment and disagree with it, supporting your statement with your material.

For example, if I suggest an income-producing technique to an audience of business people and the Heckler suggests it won't work, I would not acknowledge that statement initially. Then, when I use a compelling example of the technique working out, and I see my audience responding positively, I could say, "Do you see how this will increase your profit?" Often at such a point I will make eye contact with the Heckler so he knows I heard him earlier and am addressing him with a solution to his challenge now. Typically, the heckling will subside.

If a Heckler continues to badger you or berate your presentation to the point of becoming very disruptive, you may want to respond by indicating how these comments make you feel. Do this only one-on-one. During the next break, approach the Heckler and say, "When you say [x], it makes me feel [y]. Was that your intention?"

Surprisingly, the Heckler may not even be aware of your feelings, and eliciting some empathy may cause a halt to the behavior. Even a Heckler who was being deliberately provocative may stop once you call him or her out. Either way, a direct confrontation will often end the problem.

Manage Inattention

Chapter 10 has a number of valuable techniques that will work to keep the attention of nearly anyone in your audience. But for some audience members you'll need a few other tricks up your sleeve.

Overcome active passivity

Some Naysayers fall into the category of what Dreikurs called the discouraged people. I call them Active Passivists. "I can't do that. I'll never do that. I've tried and it's failed and what you're saying won't work." They want pity, and they want you to allow them to remain helpless by being inattentive during your presentation. Don't commiserate with them. Your attitude has to be, "You're going to get this, and I'll help you." So arrange small successes.

I was working with a woman whose grandson bought her a computer. She told me, "I have a rotary phone at home. I don't even know how to use a digital phone. I'll never learn computers. I also have no idea what to do with this mouse thing." She picked up the mouse and pointed it at the screen like a TV remote and, of course, nothing happened.

With people like this, start by making them take action. In this case, I gave directions to the grandmother one step at a time: "Grab the mouse. Put it on the table. Slide it around. Look at your screen." Then I pointed out to her what she had accomplished. "You're moving the mouse, the mouse is making the arrow move, and you're using the new technology." Within thirty seconds, she had a success.

I introduced her to the expressions she had to know ("cursor," for example, and "log in") and took her through the steps to create a password and get into the email page. Again, I pointed out what she had done. "You said you couldn't use technology. Now you're ready to send email. See: You can do this.")

Notice, I used encouragement, not praise. It's no good to say, "You're so good at this" when someone knows that's simply not true; you lose credibility. Giving encouragement at each step of the way, with each small success ("You're getting this," "You can do this"), has much more impact. Within half an hour, the grandmother looked at me and said, "Wow! This isn't as hard as I thought it was."

One of my favorite ways to achieve this effect with a large audience is by using recall questions. Every quarter of your presentation, stop and ask the audience three questions that you know they'll get right. The questions must be compelling, and the answers must be something you have taught them that they can put to immediate use. When they've given the right answers, acknowledge them. When you give the audience a small success in this way, the Active Passivists will start to see (even if they don't admit it) they are getting it.

Handle apathy

There may be people in your audience who aren't paying attention but pretend they are by inserting unrelated, unproductive comments.

It's possible you are boring them. But if you've prepared well and your message is compelling, the likelihood is they, too, fall into the Dreikurs's category of those who are giving up. They don't think whatever you're trying to put across applies to them.

At the beginning of this book, I talked about the hooks: the *whys* of your presentation. If your audience is drifting, you need to hook them back in. If there's a guy in the back hunkered over his laptop in a way that tells you he's checking his email and ignoring you, you have to say something that will show him that what you're presenting has immediate value to him in his life. You need to show him he needs to listen to *you* to get what he wants.

The best way to do this is to offer a hook to the entire audience, right then and there.

One of my favorite ways to do this is through the *agree and see if you're right* technique. After you ask a question directly related to the hook of the takeaway (or the task or the subtask), and once you've given the audience members thirty seconds to write their answers, take these few moments to approach this person directly and gently prompt him or her to write a response. Generally, you'll have made your point and the person will start writing and become re-engaged—especially if the question gets his or her attention.

Your Turn to Minimize Distractions

Most of the people who give you problems have power issues, but there are ways you can handle them or anyone else who is creating a disturbance.

Review and exercises

Items flagged with arrows require action on your part. If you are uncertain how to proceed, reread the appropriate section in this chapter.

Stop interruptions

Dealing with Talk Hogs (Experts and Know-It-Alls).

- ▶ Write in your own words how to get Experts to shine.
- ▶ Write in your own words how to give attention to Talk Hogs.

Handle negativity

Dealing with Resenters and Naysayers.

- ▶ Write the three steps to end power struggles with Naysayers.
- ▶ Write the way you deal with Resenters privately.

Dealing with Faultfinders (Gripers and Hecklers).

- ▶ Decide on the words you will use to set ground rules.
- ▶ Decide what words you will use to turn the issue back to the Faultfinder.

Manage inattention

- ▶ Describe how to handle the Active Passivist.
- ▶ Describe what to do to handle apathy.

Chapter Sixteen

CLOSE TO APPLAUSE

Move your audience to respond with enthusiasm

I was at a national health care conference a few years ago. One of the presenters finished, signed off with sincerity and warmth, and promised to stick around. The handclapping had been spirited. As they filed out, people were talking to one another and there was a feeling of energy in the room. "Wow!" someone said. "You said it!" someone else agreed. "That was an amazing presentation!"

Some months later, I returned to the same room to hear another presentation. That one ended quite differently. I didn't hear anyone say "wow." In fact, there wasn't even any applause at the conclusion, because people weren't quite certain that the presentation was over. The screen went to black, at which point the presenter merely said, "Thank you," and left the stage. There were a few awkward moments of people looking around, unsure whether it was time to go. Then they began to drift out, silently.

The presenters had equally interesting topics, good material, and polished deliveries, yet one sent the audience out the door buoyed and energized and the other let them leave feeling let down. The difference was that the first presenter knew what performers, directors, and producers—people who are always conscious of the audience—know almost intuitively: You need to put as much emphasis on the finale as on the opening of a show. How you close is critical.

Focused on overcoming their anxieties about the opener and their concerns about the core of the presentation, many presenters pay scant attention to how they will end it. But Rule the Room style is to plan to the end—and beyond. The presentation isn't over until you've met the needs of all the audience members. Do that, and they'll be saying "wow" about your presentation, too. To make that happen:

- Show that the presentation was worthwhile.
- Address any remaining questions.
- Tell the audience where they can get more information.
- Part with warm closing words.

Show That the Presentation Was Worthwhile

The classic rules for any sort of writing apply to presentations: Tell them what you're going to tell them, tell them, and then tell them what you told them. At the very end of your presentation, remind your audience:

- *What* they got.
- *Why* they would want it.

Put up the summary slide and summarize all the takeaways in one sentence. Begin the sentence with "You have just learned . . ." and complete the statement using the summary of the main hook for your presentation.

Richard, for example, told his audience, "You have just learned five strategies to create new sources of income with less risk."

In this book, there are sixteen takeaways with three or four techniques mentioned for each. The main hook of this book is "Create a customized, memorable presentation; feel more prepared and confident; and engage and entertain even the most challenging audience."

If I were to use this book as a presentation, I would close by saying, "You have just learned fifty strategies that will help you create a customized, memorable presentation; feel more prepared and confident; and engage and entertain even the most challenging audience."

This is powerful. I have seen people nodding their heads, looking at the list and realizing just how much they learned.

Notice that the *why* is now the last item in the summary. Since the why is the most compelling reason your presentation matters to your audience, you used it in your introduction. Since it gives them the rewards that matter to them—happiness, success, and freedom—you should end with it as well.

When you finish reiterating what they got and why they wanted it, your audience will leave the presentation motivated to do whatever your presentation was designed to achieve.

Address Any Remaining Questions

When you're finished summarizing the presentation, and while you're still on the summary slide of all the takeaways, make your final question request.

Ask, "What questions do you have about [the title of your presentation]?" Richard asked his audience, "What questions do you have about increasing business with new low-risk loans?"

In my case, it would be: "What questions do you have about giving an irresistible presentation?"

Wait the full seven seconds. Stand there using confident body language, swiveling your head to gaze at all the members of the audience, and wait the full seven seconds. It will be powerful for your audience, because they will now be thinking about your hook and questions they may have.

When you get a question, follow the usual procedure: Stand still, look at the person who's asking when he or she is speaking, paraphrase the question, and then reestablish eye contact with the larger audience when you give your answer. Of course, at this point, you can't do any more postponements. If you don't know an answer, tell them that, and offer a follow-up (see below).

At the very end of each answer, be sure to ask something like, "Does that help?," "Does that answer your question?," or "Did you get what you need?" if you think you'll be getting a positive response. Getting acknowledgment of how helpful the presentation was at the end of the presentation helps send people away with a positive impression.

Audiences love presenters who follow through on their promises. You promised to take all questions, and you also promised to end on time. What do you do if there are still hands in the air, or someone asks a question at the last moment that you think will go into overtime?

Avoid a statement such as, "I can see you have more questions, but we've run out of time." This indicates a disregard for the question (and questioner) and suggests you didn't have mastery over your pace. Instead, say, "I promised you I would end at two o'clock, and it's now two. For those of you who have additional questions, I'll stick around to answer them."

Look at what you've done:

- Delivered on your promise
- Shown your competence
- Given the audience even more of yourself

What better way to make a final, positive impression?

Now there are a few remaining items that can be wrapped up in moments.

Tell the Audience Where to Get More Information

You've reminded them what they got and why they wanted it, and presumably have won their trust and appreciation. Take advantage of the opportunity to make an ongoing connection, and do it correctly, when you display the final slide.

Let them know how to reach you

Avoid a heavy-handed approach such as, "If you'd like more information about [whatever you're offering], go to [name of website]. There you'll find material and information that will make you a huge success."

It's more subtle and, I believe, more effective, simply to include the contact information on the very last slide of your presentation along with the words "Thank you." Let them read the information, and assume they will contact you. This shows a lot of confidence.

What's more, chances are they're taking home your handout, which should also contain the information.

Confirm follow-ups (optional)

If you have offered to the entire group or to any individual that you will answer particular questions, provide a resource, or make a phone call, confirm at this point that you will follow through on your promise. You can make a generic statement such as "I will follow up on [the information you promised] by [specific date]."

If you have made such an offer and neglect to reaffirm that it will happen and on what date, your audience will question your credibility, so don't neglect this follow-up, particularly if you are trying to make a sale. One of the main ways to turn a prospect into a client is to convince the person that you (and thus your company) will stand behind your promises. Establishing fixed follow-up dates can help cast you both in a positive light.

Part with Warm Closing Words

Offer a sincere thank-you

When you thank your audience, give an actual, specific reason to thank them and you will seem even more sincere. Many presenters tend to thank the audience for their time, which suggests they might have been spending their time doing something more important. Instead, mention why you appreciate something they have done. For example, if they were very responsive—they were listening attentively and asking great questions—you might say, "Thank you for being such a warm audience." If they gave you some great feedback you were looking for, say so: "Thank you for your feedback."

As always, your tone is more important than the words you use. Keep your volume down, your pace normal, and your speech free of inflections.

Wish them well

Close with a pleasantry. You have to be able to read your audience. If your audience has been especially responsive, then you can add again, "If you have additional questions, stick around," which shows again you want to reach out to them. Otherwise cut directly to your closing remark.

"Have a great day" will suffice. It shows them you're done, just as if you're closing the curtains on a performance. To make sure they have no doubt, walk away from the sweet spot as soon as you've uttered your closing words.

Often, some of your audience will approach you to have a few words before you leave. Stay where you are or return to center stage and answer the individual questions you promised to handle. Meet their needs.

Oh . . . and expect some applause. It may begin when you make your pleasant final remark or when you walk away from the sweet spot. (The audience needs such a cue to begin.)

You may never have gotten applause for a presentation before, but if you've followed through on all my suggestions, now you will hear it time and again, after every amazing presentation you give.

Your Turn to Close to Applause

The final impression you make on your audience is as important as the first one. You want your audience to leave with positive feelings about you and your message so you will have succeeded in your goal of persuading, teaching, motivating, and/or inspiring them—and getting them to change their behavior as a result.

Review and exercises

Items flagged with arrows require action on your part. If you are uncertain how to proceed, reread the appropriate section in this chapter.

Show your audience that the presentation was worthwhile

- ▶ Decide on the words you will use on your summary slide.

Address any remaining questions

- ▶ Decide on the words you will use to make your final question request.
- ▶ Write what you will say if you think the question will be satisfied.
- ▶ Write what you will say if you don't know an answer.
- ▶ Write what you will say if someone asks a last-minute question that will take you into overtime.
- ▶ Decide what words will appear on your final slide.
- ▶ Write how you will handle follow-ups.

Part with warm closing words

- ▶ Decide on the words you will use to express your thanks.

▶ Decide what words you will use to signal the presentation is over.

▶ Review where to go immediately after saying your final words.

AFTERWORD

This book offers you the principles and tools that can help you do many things, among them create a customized, memorable presentation that your audience will crave; overcome your fears and become a confident presenter; and engage and entertain even the most challenging audience. To get results, you have to act on that advice.

Take a few minutes to think about where you would like to make changes. Write down the top ten areas in which this book has shown you ways to improve your presentation skills. Since research and my own experiences indicate that people can focus on only three goals at a time, I suggest you choose the three you want to incorporate in your life first. Start working on those, and once you have achieved them, work on the next three. Continue until you have achieved them all.

Begin by going over the relevant chapters and taking notes. Then follow up with the exercises and review at the end of the chapter. Dedicate at least an hour per week for twelve weeks in a row to practice.

Remember, presenters aren't born; they're made. You have all the tools at your disposal with a unique set of practical examples to make them happen for you. I have seen these efforts pay off for thousands of people with whom I've worked, and you will have that same experience.

You can Rule the Room.

ACKNOWLEDGMENTS

I would like to express my gratitude to all those who have such a meaningful place in my life:

- My Lord and Savior Jesus Christ, without whom none of this would be possible.
- Jess, the love of my life, the woman behind Rule the Room, and the only person I want beside me on life's journey with Jesus.
- Jim Teteak, my brother and the Rule the Room co-founder. You are to our enterprise as water is to plants.
- Michelle, Jada, Mia, and Cole Teteak, Jim's family; and Sue and Tom Teteak, our parents. You have been an endless source of love, support, and encouragement.
- And our son, Trey, a source of joy. May you one day Rule the Room.

For help in bringing this book to fruition, I would like to offer thanks to all the following:

- Cort Johns, for encouraging me to write this book.
- Amanda Rooker, for your patience and professionalism in guiding us through the editorial process.

- Morgan James Publishing, for your partnership and professional support throughout the publishing process.
- Peggy and Phil Deloria, for taking a chance on me.
- My coauthor Dale Burg. Your genius in writing is matched only by your humility.

I want to express my appreciation to my mentors through the years, for your wisdom and guidance.

To all the clients and presenters with whom I have worked, my sincere hope that you continue to Rule the Room.

ABOUT THE AUTHOR

Jason Teteak is the visionary founder and CEO of the premier presentation consulting firm Rule the Room, LLC.

In twenty years of working as a presenter and coach, he has trained more than fifteen thousand professionals to Rule the Room and has appeared before more than one hundred thousand people. He's won praise and a wide following for his original methods, his engaging style, and his knack for transferring communications skills via practical, simple, universal, immediately actionable techniques.

Jason first made a reputation in the medical training industry, where he was known as "the presentation coach and trainer who trains the trainers."

In response to many requests, he began to offer personalized services and quickly developed a following as a private coach and a consultant whose clientele includes elite institutions, universities, and top corporate executives.

He has developed more than fifty presentation and communication training programs ranging in length from one hour to three days that serve as the basis for this unique, practical, and comprehensive guide.

Visit www.RuleTheRoom.com to learn more.

Coauthor **Dale Burg** has collaborated on more than twenty books, including *The Geek Squad Guide to Solving Every Computer Glitch* (Touchstone) with

Robert Stephens, founder of the Geek Squad, and *The Money Club* (Simon and Schuster), a *New York Times* Business Best Seller. She most recently collaborated on Ken Kamen's *Reclaim Your Nest Egg: Take Control of Your Financial Future* (John Wiley and Sons).

ABOUT RULE THE ROOM

Rule the Room is a leading provider of communication solutions to people and organizations everywhere.

In every enterprise and all walks of life, communication skills are critical. Your success depends on your ability to persuade, inspire, teach, and motivate others.

Our belief is that good communicators are not born; they're made. Everyone has the capacity to be a great public speaker, an excellent presenter, and an exceptional leader when taught the necessary skills.

Rule the Room can teach you those skills, which can be applied in every situation, from giving a presentation to running a meeting, handling confrontation, and networking with clients.

We offer four categories of services: tailored on-site training for corporate and academic clients, online video training, public workshops, and executive coaching.

Our company works with everyone from novices to seasoned presenters. Among those we have trained are executives; technical, financial, sales, and human resources professionals; project managers; trainers and educators; and academic administrators.

We provide the gold standard of presentation curriculum for elite companies and institutions worldwide, and we specialize in developing appropriate mentoring training for the current and future leaders at your organization to prepare them to Rule the Room.

One of the many programs we offer is Presentation Bootcamp: The Complete Hands-On Presentation Skills Training Camp. It covers the contents of this book with the added dimension of live demonstrations, and provides an opportunity to work on your own presentation under the guidance and with the feedback of our staff.

A partial list of our programs is below. For a complete list and more information, visit www.RuleTheRoom.com.

- Academia: How to Give a Seamless Administrative Presentation
- Activity: Effective Tools for Facilitating Classroom Activities
- Advantage: How to Give a Compelling Business Presentation
- Ambassador: Learn to Teach Trainer Bootcamp at Your Site
- Archetype: Entertain Your Audience Using Your Unique Personality Style
- Boomerang: How to Answer Questions Like a Pro
- Bullseye: How to Teach All Learners Simultaneously
- Calm: Overcome Your Fear of Public Speaking
- Captain: Take Charge of Your Audience and Control Your Presentation
- Captivate: How to Hook Your Audience
- Clone: Learn to Teach Presentation Bootcamp at Your Site
- Coach: Learn to Do Presentation Coaching at Your Organization
- Coliseum: Techniques for Large Audiences and Classes
- Conference Call: Effectively Conduct Business over the Phone
- Convey: Deliver a Convincing Message with Confidence and Credibility
- Cram: An Accelerated Guide to Adult Learning for New Trainers
- Create: A Comprehensive Approach for Creating Compelling Presentations
- Dazzle: The Complete Guide to Delivering a Successful Presentation
- Demo: Entice Your Prospective Customers with Your Demonstration
- Eloquence: How to Convince with Your Voice
- Energy: Reduce Your Stress and Invigorate Your Life
- Expression: The Art of Body Language and Facial Communication

- Facilitate: Guide and Manage Valuable Adult Learning Discussions
- Faculty: How to Give a Compelling Lecture
- Feedback: How to Observe, Evaluate, and Give Advice about Presentations
- Five: Deliver a Compelling Five-Minute Presentation
- Foundation: The Complete Guide to Effective Adult Learning
- Hire: Get the Right Talent for Your Business
- Impress: Take Advantage of Interaction with Your Customers
- Interview: Advanced Strategies to Ace Your Job Interview
- Launch: Deliver a Killer Presentation Opener
- Lightbulbs: How to Make Things Easy to Understand
- Maintain: Engage and Hold the Attention of Your Audience
- Maverick: How to Become an Elite Trainer
- Meeting: How to Run Effective Business Meetings
- Mentor: Learn to Do Trainer Coaching at Your Organization
- Network: Use Small Talk to Get Connected
- Presentation Bootcamp: The Complete Hands-On Presentation Skills Training Camp
- Presto: Get the Instant "Wow" Factor for Your Presentation
- Productive: Get More Done in Less Time
- Recharge: Renew Your Energy and Avoid Burnout in the Classroom
- Respect: Become Recognized as a True Leader
- Respond: Elicit and Answer Questions with Ease
- Scribe: How to Develop Effective Training Curriculum
- Serenity: How to Handle Challenging People
- Trainer Bootcamp: The Complete Hands-On Train-the-Trainer Program
- Validate: How to Deliver an Effective Validation Session
- Video: How to Create Effective Training Videos for Your Content
- Virtual: Effective Methods for Online Training
- Webcast: How to Give an Effective Webinar
- Upload: How to Create and Promote a Successful Internet Video

INDEX

CPSIA information can be obtained at www.ICGtesting.com
Printed in the USA
BVOW04s1041300114

343499BV00007B/344/P